B. CAWLEY

STAND & DELIVER

My Hotel Chelsea
35 Ixworth Place
London
Chelsea
SW3 3QX

For a complete list of Management Books 2000 titles,
visit our web-site on http://www.mb2000.com

STAND & DELIVER

Mark Barnes and Mary-Jane Barnes

2000

We would like to thank everyone who has worked with us at Step System, delivering Presentation Skills, Communications or Media training - for their commitment, so generously given.

Many thanks to Julie Malik for her dedication, patience and support and to Paul Richardson for his cartooning skills. Julie's and Paul's skills have played a significant part in establishing the 'Step System style'.

Thanks must also go to Chris and Rona Thorogood for validating the physiological content of Stand & Deliver.

Finally, heartfelt thanks to Wayne Phillips and Ian Licence - great champions, sponsors and friends.

This book is dedicated to Christopher and Catie –

'If you believe you can, you can!'

First published in 2007 by Management Books 2000 Ltd
Forge House, Limes Road
Kemble, Cirencester
Gloucestershire, GL7 6AD, UK
Tel: 0044 (0) 1285 771441
Fax: 0044 (0) 1285 771055
E-mail: info@mb2000.com
Web: www.mb2000.com
Printed and bound in Great Britain by 4edge Ltd of Hockley, Essex – www.4edge.co.uk

British Library Cataloguing in Publication Data is available

ISBN 1-85252-533-9

ISBN 13 978-185252-533-0

Contents

Contents

Key to symbols used throughout this workbook

Question

Answer

Tip

Instruction

Introduction

- Getting the most from *Stand & Deliver*

- The '4 Ps'

- Making successful presentations

- Deciding on your outcomes

- The four sections of the book

- Contact us

- Developing your skills

- Presentation Skills Effectiveness Wheel

- Action plan

Getting the most

No matter what the presentation opportunity, it is imperative that you present yourself and your ideas in the most appropriate way. To do this you must have confidence that you will be able to get your message across.

You can best guarantee success as a presenter by undertaking sound preparation, by developing the skills that will fully engage your listeners and by being assured that you are in control.

With each of these success factors in place, your listeners will be more likely to understand and remember all of the points that you wanted to make and, as a result will think, do or believe something different. You and your message are going to be judged afresh on how well you handle each new presentation opportunity!

You never get a second chance to make a first impression!

Stand & Deliver is intended for business people, for individual study or to be used by coaches and trainers as a resource to support and develop presentation skills.

It has been created by practitioners and is a comprehensive journey through the key elements of presenting, containing incisive 'how-to' content, providing everything necessary to make powerful presentations – with impact!

The '4 Ps'

Stand & Deliver will help you by focussing on the '4 Ps' ensuring that you will always get the basics right. It can then be used to hone existing skills, build confidence and truly grow credibility.

$$\text{P{\small LAN}}$$
$$\downarrow$$
$$\text{P{\small REPARE}}$$
$$\downarrow$$
$$\text{P{\small RACTISE}}$$
$$\downarrow$$
$$\text{P{\small ERFORM}}$$

Making successful presentations

In our experience, most people's desire to develop their presentation skills has to do with their wanting to deliver 'successful presentations'.

Successful normally means that:

- ❑ **The presentation has gone smoothly** – there have been no personal or technical disasters and the audience seemed to be 'happy'.

- ❑ **The presenter has gained in personal credibility** – they have done themselves and their message 'justice' and were able to deal with any questions.

- ❑ **They had professional impact** – they projected a strong image of their organisation and of their own professionalism.

- ❑ **The presentation was memorable** – the audience could remember the key parts of the message and understood fully what they should 'believe, know, think or do' as a result of attending a presentation that they saw as a worthwhile investment of their time.

Deciding on your outcomes

What would you like people to say about **your presentations**, once you have given them?

_____

_____

_____

_____

What would you like them to say about **you**?

_____

_____

_____

_____

Whatever your desired outcome, every chapter of this book will be of great value to you. Remember – any presentation is really a fantastic opportunity to enhance your profile!

You can use this book as a self-help tool to further refine your skills by working through chapter by chapter. Alternatively, you can dip into any of the chapters as and when you wish, either to get information that could help you to raise your game in a particular area, or to enable you to create or add value to a specific presentation.

There are tools, tactics and tips as well as development exercises. Use the exercises – the more frequently you practise, the greater the effect and the more positive the outcome will be.

The four sections of the book

To help you, after this introduction, you will find that this book has been divided into four sections.

Section 1 is concerned with the process and tools necessary to create and deliver a presentation.

Section 2 focuses on managing yourself and aligning the contributory factors that decide whether a presenter comes across as being credible.

Section 3 focuses on the audience and what they need for the presentation to be accessible.

Section 4 deals with the unknown and the unusual – dealing with the environment, questions and 'non-standard' situations.

Contact us

If you would like further coaching or technical input around these or more advanced aspects of communication, presenting or dealing with the media from Mark, Mary-Jane or their team of colleagues, please contact them by email.

mark@stepsystem.co.uk

mary-jane@stepsystem.co.uk

www.stepsystem.co.uk

Developing your skills

Self scoring – use this chapter of the book to identify your strengths and areas for development. This will enable you to create a personal action plan.

People who deliver successful presentations focus on key success criteria. Over the page (see Figure 3) we have created a Presentation Skills Effectiveness Wheel, which captures ten of these, one per segment. Each segment corresponds to a chapter in this book.

The wheel has a scoring mechanism, which runs from 0 at the centre (the lowest score), to 10 at the outer edge (the highest score). Your personal score will fall somewhere between these two extremes!

Step 1 – think of a presentation that you have made recently. On that performance, how would you score yourself in each of the segments (see Figure 1)?

Mark and shade your score with a highlighter pen as shown in the diagram, right. Do not be tempted to score ten out of ten for everything, but use the full range of scores.

Total up the scores that you gave yourself in each segment and enter this new score into Box A over the page, headed 'current cumulative score'. Because there are 10 segments, and you are scoring out of 10, it will be represented as a percentage.

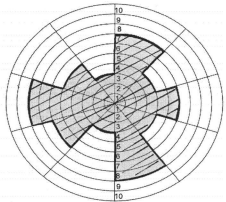

Figure 1

Step 2 – now revisit the effectiveness wheel and with a different coloured highlighter pen, identify those areas where you think either you could, or should, move the score forward (see Figure 2).

Again, be realistic. Do not assume that you can move all the scores forward to ten out of ten. Look instead for real areas of opportunity to raise your game.

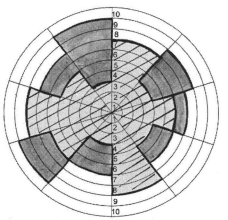

Figure 2

Once you have completed the scoring, add up the total shaded area and put this new total score into Box B marked 'target score'.

Step 3 – find the difference between Box A and Box B. This is 'The Gap', which reflects your opportunity to develop and 'raise your game'.

Presentation skills effectiveness wheel

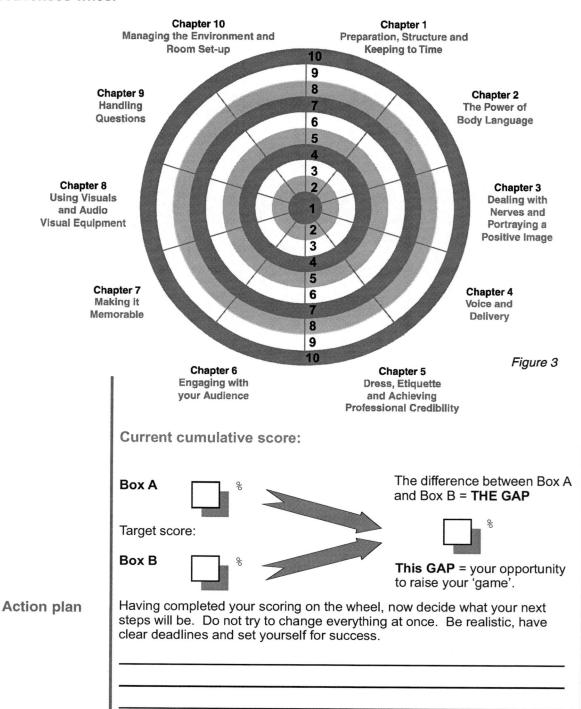

Figure 3

Current cumulative score:

Box A ☐ %

Target score:

Box B ☐ %

The difference between Box A and Box B = **THE GAP**

☐ %

This GAP = your opportunity to raise your 'game'.

Action plan

Having completed your scoring on the wheel, now decide what your next steps will be. Do not try to change everything at once. Be realistic, have clear deadlines and set yourself for success.

_____

_____

_____

Section 1

Chapter 1

Preparation, Structure and Keeping to Time

- Reviewing your current methods
- The Four Corner-stones
- Clarifying the purpose
- Know your audience
- Drawing together the content
- The X-ray Sheet
- The best medium for delivery
- Managing the introduction

- Managing the conclusion
- Managing the middle
- Completing the X-ray Sheet
- Colour coding
- Reviewing the X-ray Sheet
- Managing time
- Finishing on time
- X-ray Sheets

Reviewing your current methods

List your current methods of preparation below.

_____
_____
_____
_____
_____
_____
_____
_____
_____
_____
_____
_____
_____

What are the advantages and disadvantages of each method?

Advantages	Disadvantages

The Four Corner-stones

It has been said that a well-prepared presentation is already 90% given. This simply reflects the degree of control and confidence that comes from the certain knowledge that the presenter has prepared thoroughly and is already set for success.

When preparing and planning presentations, always consider the Four Corner-stones. Ask yourself the following questions:

Corner-stone one

Why am I making this presentation?
What is my purpose?
What is my point of view?

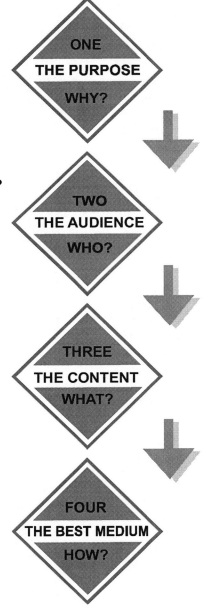

Corner-stone two

Who am I making this presentation to?
What will they need or expect from this presentation?
What are the benefits for them?

Corner-stone three

What is the relevant content?
What am I going to say?
What must I include?

Corner-stone four

How am I going to say it?
What means or methods should I use to get my message across?
What can I do to ensure that the audience will engage with my message?

It would also be sensible to temper the Four Corner-stones with the side issues of When? and Where? the event is to take place.

These additional questions will have an impact on the audience, the choice of content and the best medium through which to get the message across.

'I keep six honest serving-men (they taught me all I knew); their names are What and Why and When and How and Where and Who.'

Rudyard Kipling

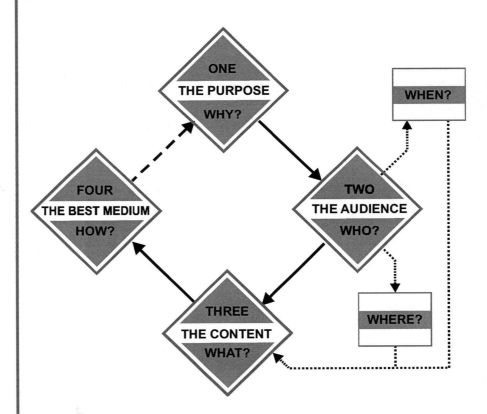

Together, these fundamentals provide the firm foundations upon which any impactful presentation can be built.

Notice that this method of preparing a presentation, does not begin by asking: 'What background shall I choose for my PowerPoint?'!

Clarifying the purpose

As a starting point, ask yourself:

- ❑ What is the purpose of this presentation?
- ❑ Why am I giving it?
- ❑ What are my intended and ideal outcomes?

It is often easy to give general answers to these questions, but your aim should be to narrow it down to a precise, single sentence purpose or objective. Without this being clear, it would be a waste of time to begin to work on what you are going to say, or to develop the mediums through which you are going to say it.

Many people get very involved in the 'how' (getting creative with their PowerPoint, for example), before they are really clear about the 'Why' and the 'What'. So, 'Why' are you making this presentation? 'What' is your purpose?

Create an objective – beginning with the words, 'I want to …' then select the appropriate 'action word' to describe what it is that you want to do.

Do you want to inform, sell, motivate, persuade or entertain? Being clear about your final outcome will provide focus.

At this early stage, clarity is all:

> *'If you don't know where you are going, any path will get you there!'*
> Rudyard Kipling

It is imperative that you check with your sponsor that your understanding of the purpose of the presentation is the same as theirs. Once you have got the purpose clear and confirmed, write it on the top of the X-ray Sheet (see page 23). You can then begin the process of deciding which ideas should, or should not, be included in your presentation – and this will depend upon a number of factors – starting with the audience.

There can be no such thing as a 'standard' or generic presentation, because no two audiences are alike. For this reason, it is essential to prepare fully by gaining any insights that you can into the audience profile.

Never overestimate your audience's knowledge, never underestimate their intelligence.'
C P Scott

Ask yourself:

❑ What is the make-up or mix of this audience?

- What will I need to do to engage everyone?
- How will I establish rapport with everyone?

❑ What will grab and interest them?

- What are their hopes, needs, expectations?
- How will I help them to answer the 'WIIFM' factor (the 'What's In It For Me?' factor)?

❑ How experienced are they in the subject matter?

- What will they already know?
- At what level should I pitch this presentation?

❑ What will they want to know or need from me?

- How will I anticipate this?
- How will I reassure them at the beginning that all will be clear by the end?

❑ Am I making this presentation for my benefit, or for theirs?

❑ Am I telling? Am I selling?

❑ How interactive do I want this presentation to be?

❑ What do I need them to believe, know, think or do differently?

If the opportunity for you to present has been created by a 'sponsor', what will they expect from your presentation? How will they have marketed it to the audience? What will you need to include in order to guarantee that all stakeholders are happy?

You might also like to consider the time of day that your presentation will take place and whether it is a component in a much larger event – the answer to both of these questions will have an effect on the audience interest levels and their attention span.

Only when you are clear about the answer to these questions, is it possible to select the most relevant material and the most appropriate mediums through which to present it.

The size of the audience will have a significant impact on the way that you structure your presentation. With small groups, there is likely to be more opportunity for interaction, whilst with larger groups the communication is more likely to be one way – unless you work hard to find ways to involve and engage with everyone.

Always remember to talk **with** your audience and not **at** them and ensure that no matter what size the group, individuals leave the presentation feeling that it has been a worthwhile investment of their personal time.

Try to mirror your audience using conventions (style of dress, choice of language, and so on...). This will make them more likely to become attuned with you and to your message (see Chapter 5).

Drawing together the content

The X-ray sheet

The X-ray Sheet offers an overview of a whole presentation at a glance (see pages 32 and 174 for completed examples). You can use the X-ray Sheet both as part of the creative process and as a safety net or prompt, during the presentation itself. It will hold the 'bare bones' of your content and show the required timings throughout.

You can also use the X-ray Sheet to check that your presentation flows, that it has a 'red thread' and contains clear transitions, as well as a good mix of input and interaction – with lots of opportunities to heighten attention and emphasise your key points.

Finally, it will give you an opportunity to review your tactics and to ensure that your approach is well thought through and is appropriate to this audience and to this occasion.

Written text flows differently from the spoken word. Writing out full text is arduous and the end result can often sound stilted. For that reason, it is really useful to identify key themes and points and then deliver them, live, in your own words.

There are lots of ways to express a single idea – as you practise your presentation, you will find the one that has a good rhythm and which flows best for you.

To get the best from the X-ray Sheet follow the guidelines below:

❑ When you need to prepare your next presentation, photocopy the blank X-ray sheet on page 23.

❑ You will need a black, blue, red and green pen, a pencil and some yellow stickies.

❑ Write the title and purpose of your presentation at the top of the X-ray Sheet in black. This will sharpen your focus and remind you exactly why you are there and what you need to communicate.

Fold-out A4-size X-ray sheet for photocopying

Step 1 – brainstorm all of the points that you could include in your presentation and capture them, one idea per sticky.

- ❑ Use one key word, or phrase per sticky – avoid writing sentences.

- ❑ Do not censor any ideas at this stage – allow your creativity to flow.

Step 2 – cluster the stickies into a maximum of four main groups and give each cluster a heading.

These columns will be your main content, sandwiched between an introduction and a conclusion.

- ❑ You will find that certain key areas of content emerge, while redundant ideas, which do not fit in, become apparent and can be thrown away.

- ❑ **So, do it!** Throw redundant or irrelevant ideas away – do not try to squeeze them in for the sake of it.

Step 3 – organise your clusters in vertical columns and distinguish between those points that you must, should and could include, a process which will be influenced by the amount of time you actually have available to deliver your presentation.

During this stage, your key 5% of content should also become apparent.

Step 4 – this information can now be transferred to the X-ray Sheet, leaving the first column free for your introductory points and the last for your summary and close (see example 1 on page 31).

Now that you are clear on your key points, it is essential to ensure that the style that you use and the mediums through which your presentation is delivered take into account the needs of the audience, whilst adding value and credibility to your message.

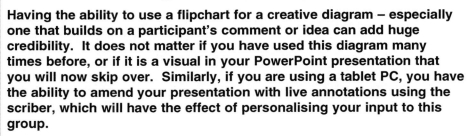

It is no good having an exciting group activity for example, if the audience will not play – or a fantastic questionnaire, if the layout of the room, or the time available, prevent it from being used to full advantage, or from being debriefed properly.

It is important to recognise your own strengths in delivery and play to those. There is no point attempting to do something which you have seen others do well, if you do not feel sufficiently comfortable with it to be assured that you will be able to get your message across on this occasion.

There may be times, of course, where you have no choice but to follow an accepted and previously established style. For example, in a conference setting, where a succession of speakers are expected to deliver PowerPoint presentations, it might appear strange if one speaker suddenly wheeled out an overhead projector, or a flipchart! Having said that, many audiences would welcome some innovation and, if appropriate, humour or even a chance to get involved and to do something completely different.

It can appear very convincing and engaging to change from a formal style of presenting, for example to move away from a lectern and give an apparently impromptu, (but in fact carefully rehearsed), speech. There is nothing wrong with building apparent spontaneity, ad-libs, or off-the-cuff remarks into a presentation – they usually work much better than set piece jokes anyway.

Do not be tempted to always deliver in the same style – allow some variety of approach – it will be more interesting for you and for the audience. However, if you have to use a medium that you are not completely comfortable with, practise with it beforehand and have a 'Plan B' in place, should either the technology or circumstances let you down.

Having the ability to use a flipchart for a creative diagram – especially one that builds on a participant's comment or idea can add huge credibility. It does not matter if you have used this diagram many times before, or if it is a visual in your PowerPoint presentation that you will now skip over. Similarly, if you are using a tablet PC, you have the ability to amend your presentation with live annotations using the scriber, which will have the effect of personalising your input to this group.

Clearly, knowing the audience and your sponsor's expectations would be useful in deciding what would, or would not, be appropriate on each occasion.

Choose the medium most appropriate to:

❑ the message

❑ the audience

❑ the tone and mood of the event

❑ the venue

❑ your own level of skills.

Then, use 'The News at Ten Approach'.

'Tell them what you're going to tell them,
Tell them,
Then tell them what you've told them.'

Managing the introduction

'Tell them what you're going to tell them ...'

Within the first few minutes of speaking, your audience will have decided whether or not they are going to bother to listen. If you lose them at this stage it will be hard to regain their attention and some of them may even become creatively difficult – so that no matter how good your preparation and content, your message will be lost!

The content of your introduction could include the following:

❑ Welcome the group.

❑ Outline your credentials:

- who you are
- your credibility – why you are the right person to make this presentation
- the purpose of your presentation – once they know why you are there and what is in it for them, they will be more likely to give you their attention
- a 'grab' to make them sit up and take notice
- an explanation of why it is important that they listen to you.

❑ Give a summary of the content.

- Let them know your agenda and time scales.
- Give them a 'route map' of where you intend to take them.
- Tell them whether you will take questions as you go, or intend to provide an opportunity and time for questions at the end.

All that you can do here is state your preference! A senior audience, or one that is not happy with the direction of the presentation, are likely to interrupt whenever they like!

Managing the conclusion

'... Tell them what you've told them ...'

The content of your conclusion should include the following:

☐ All of those points that you have made and which you most want the audience to retain the longest – in other words, the key 5% of your content.

☐ If you have promised time for questions – now is the time! Take any questions, but manage the process (see Chapter 9).

☐ Once the question session is completed, re-summarise and round things off – remind them why they have been there and what you want them to do as a result of the investment of their time – make sure that when they leave, it is your message that is ringing clearly in their ears.

Other ideas to incorporate in your close might be:

☐ a return to your opening grab

☐ a recommendation, or a 'call to action'

☐ a question for the audience to consider

☐ a request for the next step – for example, if this is a sales pitch, then incorporate a request to proceed to the next stage, or ask for confirmation that you have the business – be brave!

☐ your contact details

☐ a 'thank you' and a smile.

See example 3 on page 32.

Managing the middle

'... Tell them ...'

You have up to four columns remaining on your X-ray Sheet for your main content. If you need more columns than this, you are probably attempting to make two presentations and you should begin a second X-ray Sheet to plan out what you intend to say after you have given your audience a break!

It is imperative that you know what you are going to say and how you are going to say it – if it is not clear to you, then the audience do not stand a chance. But remember, sometimes 'less is more'!

Completing the X-ray Sheet

Use the X-ray sheet

❑ Each column should be viewed as a mini-presentation that is linked to the next, creating a logical sequence.

❑ Each column should contain between one and three Key Points, supported by subordinate points. (See example 2 on page 31.)

Colour coding

❑ These points can be colour-coded in order to prioritise them. Use:
- **black** for headings
- **red** for your 'must have' content
- **green** for 'nice to have' content
- **blue** for instructions and highlighting.

❑ Put in your title, your purpose, the column headings and key points. Add instructions to yourself, (i.e. to include a visual, story or anecdote) so that these main messages are highlighted for the audience and they are fully engaged with what you are delivering. (For more ideas, see Chapter 7). These 'highlights' add value by raising the audience's attention levels and can be coded on the X-ray Sheet, so that you can see them at a glance. (See example 4 on page 32.)

Reviewing the X-ray Sheet

❑ Once you have completed your X-ray Sheet, stand back and look at it as a whole.
- Are your sections linked? Is there a clear 'red thread' running through your presentation?
- Does the whole thing 'hang together' and flow? Have you got clear transitions from the end of one column of the X-ray Sheet to the beginning of the next?
- Are your messages clear? If 'less is more', too much detail can camouflage the key messages.
- Does your presentation interest **you**? If you are not enthusiastic about it, your audience certainly will not be!

❑ Create an agenda or 'route map' of your presentation.

- Using a flipchart, you can simply list the column headings from the X-ray Sheet to create an agenda, which the audience will be able to refer to throughout your presentation.
- Using PowerPoint, there is an opportunity to create 'tabs' in your master slide that appear down the side of every slide in the deck. Each 'tab' should contain a heading representing a main theme from the X-ray Sheet. As you deliver the presentation, the 'tab' can be highlighted to show your progress (see Appendix 2). You can still use the main body of the slides in the normal way – for bullet points, or for diagrammatic support of your key messages.

Using either a flipchart or PowerPoint 'tabs' in this way means that you as a presenter can also keep the headline structure of your presentation in sight, which acts as a good anchor point and prompt for you. For the audience, being able to see your agenda helps them to keep your key themes in mind and lets them know that you are 'on track' and making progress towards your declared end point and end time.

Managing time

Using the clock faces at the bottom of the X-ray Sheet will also enable you to manage your time allocations.

Always mark on the cumulative elapsed time (the total time that will have passed when you reach the end of that column.) Your audience will not mind if you finish early – but most people do not like it when an event overruns!! (See example 4 on page 32.)

Finishing on time

Be aware that you may be asked to reduce the length of your presentation at very short notice:

> *'Oh, the previous speaker has overrun.*
> *Can you cut your input by 20 minutes?'*

Having planned an hour-long presentation, it might be tempting to talk more quickly and to try to cram everything that you originally wanted to say into the time that is now available. This is a mistake and is very unlikely to work.

It is inevitable that your summary, your emphasis on key points, or the time promised for questions will be squeezed. Even worse, you may overrun, turning a previously enthusiastic audience into an unhappy one – leading to a loss of both impact and professional credibility.

This is where the X-ray Sheet really pays off!

Having used the colour coding to show those points that you must, should and could include, if time allows, you can now see at a glance those components (in each column) that you can most afford to cut, when your time is reduced. This means that you can edit as you present and ensures that you finish on time, every time, having delivered all of your key components.

Developing this ability to edit with confidence 'on your feet' will mean that you can cut content horizontally on the X-ray Sheet – ensuring that you will still have the key points from all of your columns, rather than being forced to cut vertically, and losing whatever happens to be in the later columns – your summary, your closing 'grab', your call to arms, or your request for the business.

Points to remember:

☐ **Use the X-ray Sheet to prepare, practise and perfect your presentation.** Allow time for a 'stumble through', a 'run through' and a dress rehearsal!

☐ **You cannot rehearse too much** – whatever your level of confidence, rehearsal, or the lack of it, will show through.

☐ **Include using visuals and handling questions in your rehearsals** – these eat up the time in a live presentation.

☐ **Each time you practise, try to use your X-ray Sheet less as a prop.** Familiarity with the content will help a natural rhythm and flow to develop. By the time you come to make your 'live' presentation, the X-ray Sheet should have done its job, but by all means keep it on hand to refer to.

☐ **Try to develop a feeling of apparent spontaneity** – you can achieve this by knowing your content so well that you are happy to include fresh or topical 'off-the-cuff' remarks, wherever appropriate.

Thorough preparation will give you the confidence to face any audience and to be adaptable to circumstance!

The great benefit of having a plan and being well-prepared and rehearsed means that you can relax into the presentation – allowing spontaneity, whilst ensuring that it still has good shape and that the key points will shine through.

Title of this Presentation: X-ray sheet – Example 1   **Purpose: Transferring Bullet Points**

Introduction	Heading	Heading	Heading	Heading	Close
	Key point	Key point	Key point	Key point	
	Key point	Key point	Key point	Key point	
	Key point	Key point			
		Key point		Key point	
⏰	⏰	⏰	⏰	⏰	⏰

Title of this Presentation: X-ray sheet – Example 2   **Purpose: Adding the 'Nice to have' content**

Introduction	Heading	Heading	Heading	Heading	Close
	Key point Example	Key point Anecdote	Key point	Key point Example	
	Key point	Key point Example	Key point Anecdote	Key point Analogy	
	Key point Anecdote	Key point		Key point Analogy	
⏰	⏰	⏰	⏰	⏰	⏰

Title of this Presentation: X-ray sheet — Example 3   **Purpose: Adding the Introduction & Close**

Introduction	Heading	Heading	Heading	Heading	Close
Welcome	Key point	Key point	Key point	Key point	Summary
You	Example	Anecdote		Example	Heading
Credibility					Heading
Purpose	Key point	Key point	Key point	Key point	Heading
"Grab"		Example	Anecdote	Analogy	Heading
Heading					Questions
Heading	Key point				Summary
Heading	Anecdote	Key point		Key point	"Grab"
Heading				Analogy	Thanks

Title of this Presentation: X-ray sheet — Example 4   **Purpose: Adding Highlights**

Introduction	Heading	Heading	Heading	Heading	Close
Welcome	Key point	Key point	Key point	Key point	Summary
You	Example	Anecdote	Analogy	Example	Heading
Credibility				Activity	Heading
Purpose	Key point	Key point	Key point	Key point	Heading
"Grab"		Example	Anecdote	Analogy	Heading
Heading	Metaphor	Analogy			Questions
Heading	Key point				Summary
Heading	Anecdote	Key point		Key point	"Grab"
Heading		Example		Analogy	Thanks
				Example	
+5 5	+15 20	+10 30	+5 35	+15 50	+5 55

Section 2

Chapter 2

The Power of Body Language

- Using your body to tell a story
- The Mehrabian Circle
- Managing your body
- Effective body language
- Align your body and mind

- Appropriate signals
- Inappropriate signals
- Make a positive start
- The Ready Position

Using your body to tell a story

Every one of us has developed the ability to 'read body language' from a very early age.

As babies and small children, we responded to a happy, smiling face more readily than we did to a scowl. As we got older we could tell if a parent or teacher was unhappy with us as they walked towards us – we did not have to wait for them to open their mouths and, as adults, we can tell fairly easily if someone is showing signs of being bored, unhappy or angry.

In the same way, when you present to an audience, they are constantly responding to the messages that are being given out consciously, or unconsciously, by your body. The audience are reading your body language – just as you, of course, can read theirs!

The Mehrabian Circle

Professor Albert Mehrabian researched spoken communication and specifically the communication of messages conveying feelings and attitudes. In his book *'Silent Messages – Implicit Communication of Emotions and Attitudes'*, he estimated that when verbal and non-verbal signals conflict:

- ❑ **7%** of the meaning is derived from the **words that are spoken**, (i.e. through **VERBAL COMMUNICATION**).

- ❑ **38%** of the meaning is paralinguistic and is derived from the **way that the words are spoken**, (i.e. through **VOCAL COMMUNICATION**).

- ❑ **55%** of the meaning is derived from **non-verbal cues** – facial expression and body language signals, (i.e. through **VISUAL COMMUNICATION**).

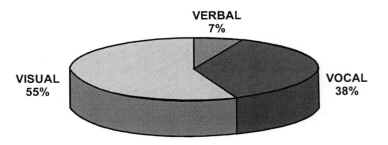

This highlights the importance of considering factors (other than words alone) when trying to convey a message as a speaker, or when attempting to interpret meaning as a listener.

Managing your body

Mehrabian's work, supported by that of Michael Argyle in his book *'The Psychology of Interpersonal Behaviour'*, clearly demonstrates that audiences are not impressed by words alone, and are greatly (even disproportionately) influenced by enthusiasm, vitality and sincerity. This information, if it is handled proactively, can really become a potent weapon in a presenter's armoury.

Effective body language

From this it is clear that effective body language adds value to the message, allowing the presenter to project a stronger and more confident image. Audiences will respond better to a presenter whose body is 'alive' and energetic, and they will appreciate movement which is meaningful and supportive to the message that is being conveyed. For this reason, the most effective movements must be those which reflect the presenter's personal investment in their message.

This is further highlighted when two presenters have to deliver similar content. The distinguishing factor in why one's delivery is more successful than the others has to do with the individual's ability to connect with the words and bring them to life. It is noticeable that those presenters who care deeply about their content and who are passionate, will unconsciously use their entire bodies to support the message that they want to convey.

Be aware of your body language and how it might be interpreted by others. If you want your verbal message to be accepted, then your *gestures, behaviour* and *voice* must all be congruent and as convincing as the words that you choose to use – any movement or vocal inflection that does not add to your presence, detracts from it.

Align your body and mind

Appropriate signals

It is a short step to eradicate unhelpful signals and replace them with powerful positive signals. Working on these will enable you to be more personally engaging and your presentations to be more persuasive.

You are your own best visual aid, so build on your strengths and allow your natural self to shine through! Your gestures can show enthusiasm and confidence. They add life to a presentation, add fluency to delivery and emphasis to words and feelings. Ignore them at your peril!

Non-verbal clues to develop:

❑ **Begin with a strong and controlled stance** – stand up straight and to your full height. This will convey your confidence and will lend an air of authority to your opening piece. How you stand at the front of the room will send a resounding message (you are happy, scared, confident or uncomfortable), long before you open your mouth. Having a firm stance also serves to keep random body movement and distracting mannerisms in check and to disguise any outward signs of nervousness (see The Ready Position, on page 40).

❑ **Work your face** – the movement of your eyes, mouth, and facial muscles can build a connection with your audience by conveying your positive feelings. Try to unfreeze your face right from the start and allow it to convey your passion.

❑ **Make good eye contact** – no part of your facial expression is more important in communicating sincerity and credibility than your eyes. With smaller groups effective presenters engage with one person at a time – focusing long enough on an individual to complete the delivery of a natural phrase and to watch it sink in for a moment – rather like a golfer watching a ball that has left the putter and is tracking all the way into the hole. With larger groups, it is useful to make eye contact with 'blocks' of the audience in order to include as many people as possible.

Eye contact should be both confident and random. It demonstrates your willingness to connect with the audience and displays both openness and sincerity.

"... AND I HAVEN'T EVEN STARTED YET!"

Eye contact draws people in, encouraging audience involvement and gives you the opportunity to check that the audience is still with you. This level of focus really works, because it demands the attention of the audience – drawing the eyes of each individual and creating natural pauses between phrases. These pauses in themselves boost attention and also contribute significantly to the understanding and retention of the key points, because they allow the listeners sufficient time to process the message.

❑ **Remember to smile** – this will have the effect of lightening the atmosphere and relaxing the listeners. Combining a smile with strong eye contact (and perhaps an encouraging nod) makes it very likely that you will receive a smile and other positive signals back!

❑ **Use humour whenever it is appropriate** – this will help you to engage with the audience and help them to 'tune in' to you and your message.

❑ **Use 'open' and expansive gestures** – use your hands to help emphasise a point, express emotion, release tension, and to engage with your audience. Most people have a wide 'gestural' vocabulary at their disposal and by using your visual communication skills you can create pictures and add emphasis or clarity to your message. In presentations it is important to scale-up gestures, making them large enough to embrace a room full of people.

The most effective gestures are from the shoulder – rather than the wrist or elbow – because these release more of the presenter's energy, and as a side-effect combat any tension that may have built up in the upper body.

❑ **Opening your arms whilst asking questions** – will demonstrate that you are genuinely open to a response. Taking feedback whilst letting your hands fall to your sides shows that you are in repose and this, allied with other 'listening body language' (leaning into the audience, angled head, nodding, thoughtful expression, smiling eyes…), will help the audience to feel able to join in.

These moments of stillness between gestures also have the effect of amplifying the gestures that you do make.

❑ **Look for opportunities to make movement with purpose** – consider using different areas of the presentation space to support different aspects of your presentation. For example, you might link standing in one part of the room to the positive aspects of your presentation, whilst returning to another area, where you have previously explained the negatives, will let the audience know that you are about to give the contrary argument.

❑ **Look for variety** – avoid being static at one extreme, or making repetitive and metronomic movement at the other. On occasions, it might be useful to advance into the audience, for example to add emphasis, or to move close to your screen to link yourself to your key PowerPoint message.

Similarly, working the audience, making contact with the 'orphans in the wings', moving to use different visual aids or props which prevent you from being static, will all keep the audience alert and interested.

Inappropriate signals

Remember to punctuate movement with stillness. Too much movement can be distracting. Constant motion, such as swaying, is a distraction that can annoy your listeners and as with gestures, these moments of stillness will provide contrast to the 'movement with purpose' that you do make.

Non-verbal clues to avoid:

❑ **Not dressing to suit the audience** – this is a mine-field and researching the audience in advance can really help here! In some circumstances, being too informal can appear to demonstrate a lack of respect, whilst in others being overly formal can make the presenter appear pompous, patronising or superior in approach. (For more information on dress and grooming, see Chapter 5.)

There is room here for some latitude around personal style – but in the business environment, conforming with the cultural norms is advisable and is also good etiquette. (For more information on etiquette, see Chapter 5.)

As a guide, the more senior the audience, the more sensible it is to err on the side of formality.

❑ **Poor posture, hands in pockets, swaying and pacing, leaning** – can all look overly-casual and transmit a message that the speaker is lackadaisical, or does not care. With some audiences (senior or older groups particularly) this will create so much 'mental interference' that they will not be able to listen to you, or to your message.

Not getting this right can be actively damaging and might well negate much of your earlier preparation and planning.

❑ **Making too little eye contact** – or reserving eye contact for your notes can suggest that the speaker lacks confidence in what they are saying – whilst looking at the ceiling or out of the window may demonstrate a lack of interest in the subject, or a reluctance to connect with the audience.

❑ **Making too much eye contact** – giving a disproportionate amount of eye contact to a few individuals, or allowing it to become too lingering, can be very disconcerting for the recipient, distracting for the rest of the audience and counter-productive for the presenter.

❑ **Forgetting to smile, being deadpan** – unfortunately, under the pressure of making a presentation, many people lose their facial expression – preventing the audience from picking up that their message is positive, or worth listening to!

By allowing the face to 'solidify' and the mouth to become a thin straight line, the tone, the mood and the energy of the presentation will all be detrimentally affected. At best, not smiling will suggest that you are nervous and at worst, that you either do not believe in your message, or simply do not want to be delivering it.

❑ **Using inappropriate humour** – a poorly judged joke or comment can easily offend and may lead to the audience feeling uncomfortable or negative. Whilst not recommending 'set piece' humour, it is important to make sure that any humorous comment is relevant to the audience – do not be tempted to 'play' to one particularly responsive section or group. Often, aiming a joke at oneself, rather than at others, can be a good tactic – but do not overplay it!

❑ **Using closed or unwelcoming gestures** – will 'turn the audience off' and any outward signs of tension through erratic gestures will transmit a feeling of awkwardness, which again is likely to transmit to the audience.

Starting a presentation by displaying positive body language – which comprises gesture, stance and facial expression – will help you to set yourself for success.

To take control, you need to be big, expressive and powerful – which demands awareness, effort and energy, as well as skill and practice.

Make a positive start

Always adopt a strong and positive demeanour, as this will send a positive message to the brain and provide the audience with an image of you as a controlled and confident presenter – despite any remaining nerves that you may actually have!

The Ready Position

The Ready Position provides a balanced stance and sends a message that you are ready to engage with the audience.

- ❑ **Stand with your feet comfortably apart, pointing straight ahead** – about shoulder width should be right – with your weight evenly distributed, but slightly forward.

- ❑ **Unlock your knee joints.**

- ❑ **Relax your shoulders** – imagine taking off a very heavy overcoat.

- ❑ **Loosen your arms and hold them by your sides** – your arms are now free to move to open gestures.

- ❑ **Touch a fingertip to thumb, or allow a fingertip to rest gently on your thigh** – this will eliminate any unnecessary fiddling and will signal to the brain that you are in control.

- ❑ **Lift your gaze towards the audience** – rather than the floor or your notes … and try a smile with eyes and mouth to signal that you are happy to be there!!

Using the Ready Position will enable you to control your body and disguise any signs of initial nervousness. It will further help by providing the ideal posture for 'open' breathing and voice production (see Chapter 4).

Return to the Ready Position whenever you need to recover or regain your composure. Use it as an anchor point, from which you can always re-centre and make a fresh start, with confidence.

As you finish your presentation, make it clear through language that you have come to an end, then smile while gently putting your hands together – with this simple movement you are quite likely to prompt the audience to give you a round of applause – a clear signal to everyone in the room that this has been a great presentation …

… and a worthwhile investment of their time!

Section 2

Chapter 3

Dealing with Nerves
and Portraying a Positive Image

- Signs of nervousness

- What is stress?

- Fight or Flight?

- The positive side of stress

- Positive thinking

- Positive visualisation

- Positive self-talk

- Freeing tension

- Positive preparation

- "I'd rather die than make a presentation!"

- Common concerns and practical solutions

Stand & Deliver

Signs of nervousness

In your experience, what are the signals that a person gives out when they are nervous?

_____

_____

_____

Which of these signals do you display?

_____

_____

_____

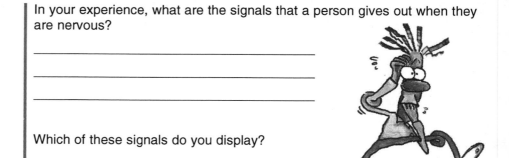

Many people find giving a presentation to be an extremely stressful situation, so you will not be alone if you feel nervous. In fact, when questioned, a large number of people put their personal fear of giving a presentation above their fear of dying!

Any presenter will sometimes feel apprehensive. Being able to manage these feelings is an important factor in giving powerful and convincing presentations. Some stress is good – it heightens awareness and speed of thinking, and will keep the presenter on their toes. Unfortunately, many people allow their nerves to get the better of them and they begin to actively communicate how nervous they feel.

Once an audience has a suggestion that the presenter is nervous, uncomfortable or not fully in control, they will look for other proof to support their interpretation. They might begin to wonder if the presenter is confident in their material and will become restless.

When the adrenaline is beginning to flow, it is important to harness this fantastic energy source and first stage of stress to your own advantage, because it will actually add vitality and spark to your presentation.

What is stress?

Stress is both a physical and mental response to one's surroundings that has evolved as a means to protect and support our wellbeing. The body constantly adjusts to our environment to keep body conditions – our metabolism – stable. This stress response is often referred to as 'Fight or Flight'.

Fight or Flight

The body prepares for physical action in order to face up to, or run away from, a perceived danger. This response was perfectly reasonable for cavemen; however the same symptoms are not so useful in a business scenario! The good news is that as it is **our** response to the situation, **we** are in a position to control it and use it to our advantage.

Symptoms of Fight or Flight – in order to manage the process, we need to recognise what is happening in our bodies and learn how to override the extreme physical response.

A stress response begins in the brain's hypothalamus, which is a structure at the base of the brain that regulates the main body functions, including appetite, body temperature and the release of hormones. Under stress, it starts the release of stress hormones (mainly adrenaline).

This is characterised by a variety of responses.

- **Eye pupils dilate and eyes widen** – leading to the 'frightened rabbit' look.

- **The muscles tense** – our knees lock and our arms feel as though they are no longer our own.

- **Heart rate increases and blood pressure rises** – blood is diverted away from some 'unnecessary organs', which we may feel as 'butterflies' in the stomach, or as cold hands and feet.

- **Blood sugar rises** – eating sensibly before your presentation will help to counteract this.

- **Body temperature rises** – we begin to sweat more freely.

- **Breathing quickens and becomes more shallow** – which can affect voice quality (see Chapter 4).

- **There is an overwhelming urge to go to the toilet.**

Taking a few deep breaths will help to break this cycle and to restore calm, as this sends the message back to the brain that we are back in control and that the panic (the need for Fight or Flight) is over.

The positive side of stress

Not all stress is bad. Without stress we would have little motivation and energy. Just as well-managed stress helps athletes to break records, it will give you an 'edge' in front of your audience.

'It is okay to have butterflies, but at least get them to fly in formation!'

Positive thinking

Positive visualisation

Positive self-talk

Freeing tension

It is sometimes useful to remember that the audience actually wants you to succeed!

An audience is very **unlikely** to have arrived wanting you to be boring, hoping that you fail to get your message across, or waste an hour or two of their time. They are much more likely to be on your side!

Before the event, try to visualise it positively: picture an enthusiastic audience, who are enjoying your presentation; notice their positive body language and enthusiastic responses and imagine yourself making eye contact and establishing a positive rapport with each one of them. They are pleased to be at your presentation and are attentive to your points, taking notes and laughing at the bits they are supposed to laugh at!

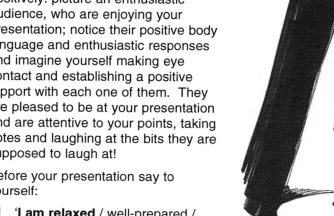

Before your presentation say to yourself:

❑ '**I am relaxed** / well-prepared / enthusiastic …'

❑ '**They are positive** / interested / receptive …'

❑ '**My presentation will be enjoyable** / stimulating / clear / memorable …'

Freeing tension 1

❑ Sit in an upright position.

❑ With your legs uncrossed, place your hands, palms down, on your thighs.

❑ Close your eyes.

❑ Imagine that any tension you find in your body is like a piece of ice.

❑ Working from your head down to your feet, find the areas of tension and melt the ice.

❑ Drain the liquid / tension out of your body, through your feet.

Freeing tension 2

❑ Sit, stand or lie down on the floor.

❑ Breathe as low down in your body as you can.

❑ Think of an area around your waistband or from your belt buckle to the small of your back and locate your breathing there.

❑ Release any tension, particularly in the head, neck and shoulders.

❑ Without forcing, breathe gently in and out – keeping the breath low.

❑ Each time you breathe out, feel you are letting the breath go out lower and lower in your upper body.

❑ Repeat, until you feel calm and relaxed.

Other tactics – simply by smiling you will come to feel more relaxed as you fool the brain into thinking that all is well in your world.

Chewing on your saliva, or an imaginary sweet, encourages the brain to think that you are taking food on board – something you are unlikely to do if you are really stressed!

Remember: the best way to overcome your nerves is to ensure that you are comfortable with your presentation – through thorough planning, preparation and rehearsal.

Positive preparation

Before the event – take responsibility for your own success. A lot of stress can be caused by uncertainty, or a feeling of being under-prepared.

In order to be assured of the veracity of what you are going to say and do:

❑ Use the Four Corner-stones.

❑ Use the X-ray Sheet.

❑ Make use of some of the later chapters in this workbook (dealing with dress, room layout or handling questions for example), to ensure that you really are 'set for success'.

❑ Rehearse, so that you feel in control.

At the event – try to find time and a private place before you begin your presentation, to prepare yourself.

❑ Adapt some of the exercises outlined above, or simply walk about and shake any excess tension from your limbs. If that is not possible then in a sitting position, work your way around your body, alternately tensing and releasing sets of muscles, while you are waiting to start. It is possible to do this without anyone else noticing.

❑ Take a few deep breaths.

❑ Try to say (or sing) a few words out loud, so that you have also exercised your vocal muscles (see Chapter 4).

'I'd rather die than make a presentation!'

There has been a lot of research carried out into public speaking and, although figures vary, there is no doubt that it is generally recognised as one of many people's greatest phobias – which if not addressed can cause high levels of anxiety.

One strategy would be to avoid having to make presentations – but business reality suggests that a more useful approach is to tackle it by:

❑ **dealing with the causes** – through preparation, planning and practice.

❑ **dealing with the outward symptoms** – through the exercises in this and the next chapter, and tactics outlined in later chapters.

❑ **further protect yourself by identifying potential stressors** – and making sure that you have a plan in place to deal with them.

Imagine that you are about to make a presentation. What are the things (situations, behaviours in others) that are most likely to cause you to feel stress?

_____

_____

_____

_____

_____

What can you do to either avoid or manage these feelings and to set yourself for success?

_____

_____

_____

_____

_____

_____

_____

_____

Common concerns and practical solutions

Common concerns	Practical solutions
• You think that you will forget what you want to say, or are worried that you might dry up in mid-sentence. • You think that you will not appear to be relaxed, that you will 'colour up', or look nervous. • You think that you have too much material and might over-run. • You think that you might run out of material.	• The key is in sound preparation and rehearsal. • Make yourself feel as comfortable as you can – prepare well, practise fully, set up your room in advance and check all of your equipment. • Do some relaxation exercises. Give yourself some positive self talk. • Use the Ready Position, breath and remember to smile! • Keep your notes to hand – be prepared to edit green content as you go.
• You think that the audience will be bored and that your content might be pitched at the wrong level. • You think that the audience might lose interest, talk amongst themselves or even walk out.	• Know your audience – do your research. Make sure your content is up-to-date and relevant. • If it is not relevant – cut it. Look for opportunities to add value and 'magic'. • Maintain good eye contact and work proactively to build rapport. • Remain positive and enthusiastic.
• You think that the audience will ask questions outside of your brief. • You think that the audience will be hostile. • You think that they might heckle or want to argue with you.	• Be clear as to why you are there – what are the parameters of your presentation? • Know your sponsor – if your presentation matches the brief and delivers the required outcomes, then you are delivering the right material – be confident! • Remain polite and courteous. • Recognise apparent expertise and defer to experience. • Throw difficult questions open to the audience for debate and then manage the discussion. • Do not be afraid to take issues off-line, or to commit to get back with an answer at a later date.
• You think that you might be let down by technology. • You are not sure how to set up or use the equipment correctly. • You think you may not have time to check the equipment.	• If technology is a potential stressor for you, either learn how to use it beforehand, get help from a colleague or the staff at the venue, or do not use it at all. • Have a 'Plan B' – if you are using PowerPoint or an OHP, be prepared to use a flipchart instead. Have graphs and tables prepared to hand out, if necessary.

Section 2

Chapter 4

Voice and Delivery

- Using your voice
- Improving posture
- Improving deportment
- Breathing properly
- Sound and words
- Vocal variety
- Tone
- Range
- Pitch
- Pace
- The value of pausing
- Diction and enunciation
- Voice projection
- Non-words and gap fillers
- Precision and control
- Keep in good voice

Using your voice

Being aware of your voice, its strength, tone and quality, and being able to manage it effectively, will have a dramatic effect on the levels of confidence that you appear to have.

As we have seen from Chapter 2, it is not so much the words that count, but the way in which they are delivered that enables the presenter to connect with the audience. Allowing your true personality (a word which derives from the Latin *per sona – through sound*) to shine through, will make an audience believe in your competence and make them want to listen to what you have to say.

❑ **Adopt a clear, well paced and energetic voice** – as well as making you easy to listen to, this demonstrates your own interest and commitment, making it more likely that you will generate the same from within the audience.

Avoid:

❑ **Monotonous, flat or one-paced delivery** – this can be hard to follow – and will suggest that the speaker himself is dull, bored and disinterested. Variety will energise and enthuse the audience. It is worth working on these.

❑ **Non-words, or 'catch-phrases', jargon and acronyms** – can be confusing, divisive and may serve to distract or exclude the audience.

Speaking is the physical process of communicating your thoughts and this happens through the instrument that is your body. Correct posture and having the ability to breathe properly are essential components in producing a full and free voice. It is impossible to use the voice to its full capability if either posture or breathing are not managed well.

Improving posture

Posture guidelines

Try to focus and:

❑ **be relaxed and natural** – keep your movements fluid.

❑ **keep your chin level, your knees loose, your head up and your shoulders sloping and relaxed.**

❑ **keep your toes pointed forward, with your weight on the heels and soles** – but be ready to move onto the balls of your feet when you begin to present.

❑ **keep the front of your neck loose** – do not stretch it, keep the abdominal muscles and your back muscles relaxed.

❑ **smile with your eyes *and* mouth!**

Try some of the following development exercises to work on your posture:

Posture 1

- Release tension by stretching your arms towards the ceiling – 2 or 3 times.

- Stand with your feet shoulder width apart. Spread your weight evenly.

- Let your arms hang by your sides.

- Look forward to an imaginary horizon.

- Lift your shoulders towards your ears and then drop them.

- Repeat this several times and feel your shoulders drop back into position, lower than when you started the exercise.

Posture 2

- Check that your spine and neck are in line and as vertical as possible. Use a mirror to guide you, or stand against a wall with as much of your back touching as is comfortable.

- When you are happy that you are standing upright, check for tension.

- Unlock any stiff joints – shoulders, elbows, knees, ankles, feet and so on.

- Let your head drop onto your chest by relaxing your neck muscles.

- Gently, roll your head across your chest – right and back centre, left and back centre.

- Repeat several times, or until you feel your neck muscles are very free.

- Now stand in an upright position – free from unwanted tension.

Improving deportment

The following exercises are used by teachers of deportment to help performers achieve correct posture. Using them will help you to become more aware of how your body works, enabling you to move with increased fluidity, whilst giving you the opportunity to correct any mistakes, as you feel them happening. Take one exercise at a time, perhaps moving on to the next one at a later date.

For these exercises, make sure that you wear loose, comfortable clothing and have flat shoes, or bare feet. You will need a long mirror, a largish book of medium weight, space enough to walk several paces and either a colleague – who can observe and give feedback – or a video camera with which you can film yourself.

Stand facing the mirror. Notice how you stand and compare this with the Ready Position (see page 40) and posture guidelines (see page 50). Make any adjustments to your posture that you feel are necessary.

Now walk towards the mirror observing your posture and movements. Remember, all movements should be fluid and your breathing natural, with your weight mainly on the balls of your feet and your heels just lightly touching the floor – the majority of movement should be from the hips and legs. The upper body should remain straight, relaxed and should not sway from side-to-side.

Now try one of the following exercises:

Posture and deportment 1

Place the book centrally on the top of your head. Turn your head slowly to the left, then to the centre and then to the right. The head movements should be smooth with eyes ahead, chin level, head, neck and shoulders relaxed. If the exercise is done correctly, the book will remain in place. Repeat this exercise until you can turn your head several times, without the book falling.

Posture and deportment 2

Place the book centrally on the top of your head and walk normally towards the mirror, observing your posture as you walk. If your posture is correct and your movements are smooth, then the book will remain in place. Repeat this exercise until you can walk the length of the space, without the book falling.

Posture and deportment 3

Place the book centrally on the top of your head and walk normally towards the mirror, observing your posture as you walk. Turn and walk back to your starting point. As before, if your posture is correct and your movements are smooth, then the book will remain in place. Repeat this exercise until you can do it without the book falling.

Breathing properly

Having good posture and carrying yourself well will make it easier for you to breathe properly. This is important because you can only speak as well as you breathe. In turn, improved breathing will reduce tension in the neck and shoulders, which, unless tackled, would also inhibit your natural voice.

We are born with the ability to breathe correctly, but as we grow older it is easy to fall into bad habits, only using the upper part of the lungs and taking shallow breaths. This can lead to breathlessness and strain in the voice. To counteract this, all presenters should learn, or relearn, how to use their diaphragm.

The diaphragm is a muscle between the lungs and the abdominal cavity. Contracting this muscle causes us to breathe in and relaxing it allows air to escape from the lungs (exhaling). So, if we control our diaphragm, we can control our inhalation and exhalation.

Good control of the diaphragm will mean that more air is available to us, for longer. Remember ... the diaphragm does not exhale for you; it just helps to control the amount of air that is exhaled.

Think of your voice as a wind instrument – using the following exercises will help to ensure that it is in tune!

Notice your breathing 1

Notice how you are breathing. Is it quick, shallow or confined to the chest area?

- Set yourself in the Ready Position (see page 40) or remind yourself of the posture guidelines (see page 50).

- Take a few deeper breaths and consciously relax. This will restore the oxygen balance in your body and will calm your whole system down.

Notice your breathing 2

Look in a mirror and take in a breath. Do your shoulders and chest rise? They should not.

- Set yourself in the Ready Position (see page 40) or remind yourself of the posture guidelines (see page 50).

- Place your hand on your stomach and try to move your breathing away from your chest. You should feel some movement in and out.

- As you exhale, release your shoulders, relax your neck, and unclench your teeth.

- Stretch out your arms and let out a big yawn.

Locating breath

- Lie on your back, or sit in an upright position and place the palm of your hand on your belly button.

- Locate your breathing in the area from the belly button to the small of your back.

- Gently, breathe in through your nose and out through your mouth.

- As you breathe in, feel a pressure all round your middle that pushes your hand up and stretches the small of your back. Do not force this.

- Pant, like a dog and feel a stronger movement.

- Relax and breathe normally.

Diaphragmatic breathing 1 – controlling breath

- Lie on your back, or sit in an upright position and place one hand over your belly button.

- Slowly inhale one long breath through your mouth and silently count to 4.

- Your stomach should expand, pushing your hand forward – your shoulders and chest should not move.

- Feel your hand move out as you pull the breath deep into your lungs.

- Hold that breath and silently count to 4.

- Breathe out through your mouth, whilst counting silently to 4.

- Check for tension, particularly in your head, neck and shoulders.

- Keep going until you are breathing easily – now repeat the exercise, steadily increasing the count up to 12.

Once you have mastered the diaphragmatic breathing exercise, you are ready to make sound.

Diaphragmatic breathing 2 – adding sound

- This time, as you breathe out, make a gentle 'Ha' sound – using the entire breath for that one sound.

- Allow the 'Ha' to stretch to 'Haaaaaaaaaa…', until you run out of air.

- Repeat this process, making sure that you really open your mouth as you sustain the sound.

Now you can begin to work on releasing tension.

Diaphragmatic breathing 3 – shoulder bounce

- This time, as you breathe out, and stretch the 'Haaaaaaa…', until you run out of air, lift your shoulders up towards your ears, hold them and only let them drop and fully relax, just as you finish making the sound and run out of air.

- Repeat a few more times.

This will release tension from your vocal chords and help you to prepare your voice to speak. It also serves to release other bodily tension – bringing obvious physical benefits – and will help your mental preparation, by reducing any anxiety that you may be feeling.

Gaining control of your breathing – 'Interrogators'

Try the following exercise with a partner. It will help you to focus on your speed and depth of breathing.

- Partner A fires questions at Partner B.

- The questions can be as demanding as Partner A likes and Partner B does not have to tell the truth in replying.

- However, before answering, Partner B consciously breathes in, then starts to breathe out and only then begins to speak.

- There will appear to be an unnaturally long pause.

- Partner A should check for apparent 'nerves' – shallow breathing, tightness in neck, shoulders, a tension in face – and that Partner B is speaking only when breathing out.

Sound and words

Sound and words 1

Sound starts with the breath. For this exercise you will need a piece of text to read aloud (a poem, some Shakespeare or a piece of fiction).

To start:

- Go into a full stretch and yawn – feel the yawn coming from the centre of your body.

- Sigh out – again feel the sigh coming from deep in your body.

- On one breath, try counting from 1 to 6 in a whisper.

- Repeat the exercise adding a little more voice each time.

- Keep linking the sound to the breath – do not strain.

- Now speak your text aloud.

- Speak it with a whisper at first, gradually add more voice.
- Make sure you take enough breath to support each word or phrase.
- Do not worry about sense – just explore the sound you can make.

Sound and words 2

Clarity of words is essential for understanding and a strong accent is not a problem – as long as the words are clear.

- Exercise your lips with the P, B, M sounds.
- Exercise the tongue, lips and jaw – they shape the words.
- Push the tongue round the inside of the mouth to exercise its muscles.
- Stroke open your jaw with your hands to release tension.
- Relish the sound that words make.
- Repeat with a piece of text for clarity and understanding.

Vocal variety

To achieve variety and interest in your voice, you should vary your tone, range, pitch, pace, and volume, just as you would in normal conversation or when reading a child a story. The best way to achieve this during a presentation is to be enthusiastic about your subject.

Remember, a monotone is monotonous! Your listeners will pick up additional cues as to how excited you are about your content and about being with them from your voice. If you are not enthused by your subject, your audience is very unlikely to be!

Common faults:

❑ **Mumbling** – it is better to be too loud, than too quiet.

❑ **Hesitating** – excessive pauses, usually filled with: '...er...' or '...um...' – pre-planning and rehearsal can often correct this.

❑ **Gabbling** – slow down; remember to breathe and to pause!

❑ **Catch phrases** – 'the point is...', 'that sort of thing...', 'you know what I mean?' – harmless in themselves, but they can become distracting for the audience (especially if they start to count them!). 'Okay?'

❑ **Dropping the voice** – allowing the voice to tail off at the end of each sentence has a boring and deadening effect.

It takes a lot of practice to appear natural in front of an audience. When you first attempt to expand your voice, it may sound false to you, but the audience will probably find it far more interesting than if you had not bothered!

Practise, practise, practise

❑ **Practise reading a variety of texts aloud.** Try a complex and dry text and then, for contrast, try a thriller and make a real effort to capture the excitement and tension. Even with dense and technical texts, search for variety. You will notice that the more complicated the text, the more you have to understand it yourself if you are to allow yourself to be expressive.

❑ **Take a piece of text and experiment with reading it in the style of:**

• a police officer reading a statement in court

• a politician giving a speech

• someone who is bored to tears

• a drowning person crying for help

• speaking full of innuendo and double meaning.

❑ **Try reading stories to children.** This offers a great opportunity to practise extending the range of your voice to an appreciative and often very encouraging audience!

Remember: if you use repetitive speaking patterns, you run the risk of losing your listeners' attention.

Tone

Tone of voice 1

Say: 'oh' with...

- anger
- polite interest
- indifference
- pity
- disgust

- great surprise
- irritability
- exhaustion
- sarcasm
- enthusiasm

Tone of voice 2

Say: 'I enjoyed your talk' ...

- enthusiastically
- as a simple statement
- with surprise
- as a statement suggesting you used to enjoy his/her talks

- as a question
- with forced politeness
- with sarcasm

To add authority and certainty, drop the tone of your voice at the end of a sentence, unless it is a question.

Range

- Sit comfortably and starting in your normal tone of voice, work down the scale singing 'Ding, dong, ding, dong!'

- Keep going until you reach the lowest note.

- Finally, work your way back until you reach your normal tone.

- Repeat this several times a day and you will find that the range of notes that you can cover will widen and your voice will become more flexible, varied and more interesting to listen to.

DING!
DONG!

Pitch

Practise making the pitch of your voice go higher and lower:

```
                                                    higher.
                                            and
                                      higher
                              voice
                        my
                  pitch
            can
      I
            can
                  pitch
                        my
                              voice
                                    lower
                                          and
                                                lower.
```

Pace

When you make your presentation, you may be tense, but the audience probably is not. Your brain might be on fast forward and it is easy to allow the mouth to catch the bug! If you are excited (whether in a positive or negative way), the spaces between your words are likely to be edited out, so you will need to press the pause button, s p a c e o u t what you are saying and S L O W D O W N !!

The value of pausing

If you can slow down, **you get**:

❑ **enhanced credibility** – it shows that you are thinking about your message and will therefore lend it greater authority.

❑ **time for you to gather your thoughts.**

❑ **an opportunity for the audience to respond and for you to gauge their feedback.**

❑ **emphasis to your key points** – people remember information with space either side.

❑ **a chance to catch your breath, re-focus and establish fresh impetus.**

Try pausing for two beats at the end of each sentence. This will inject energy and enthusiasm into the following sentence.

If you slow down, **your audience gets**:

- [ ] **time to take in your message** and think about it
- [ ] **time to check the agenda** and see where they are
- [ ] **the opportunity to respond,** or add a witty comment, without having the feeling that they are interrupting your flow
- [ ] **enhanced recall** – they will remember more if they have not had to make an effort to keep up with you, but instead had a chance to reflect and make connections whilst you are talking.

The audience might also be saved from the feeling that you have heard this all before and are simply going through the motions, before finishing and escaping as soon as possible!

Diction and enunciation

Speaking clearly will enable the audience to understand you. If your delivery is too quick, or your words are clipped, it will be hard work for them to listen and some will just give up.

This does not mean that you have to deliver like a Shakespearean actor – your usual voice, well managed, will be fine.

Vowel sounds

OO	OH	AW
AH	AY	EE

Consonant sounds

Th	S
D	T
M	N
K	G
B	P
F	V
S	Z
H	L
J	Ch
Qu	C
R	L
W	Y

Voice projection

❑ **Projection is not just about volume** – it is about adding impact by giving energy to words.

❑ **Always aim to project your voice to the back of the room** – if it is impossible to do this without deafening the front row, you may need to consider using a microphone.

Any of these voice exercises will encourage your voice to be more flexible and responsive to the demands placed upon it and with practice you will become increasingly versatile. For this reason whenever you can, speak your presentation aloud at least once and, if possible, in the size of space you will be delivering in.

Non-words and gap fillers

Ask others for feedback and identify the non-words that you use to fill silences. You may be the last person to spot them! Resist the temptation to fill your gaps. Otherwise, the message that the audience will take away – because it is the one they have heard most – may be 'um', 'er', or 'basically'!

You could begin by videoing yourself talking and then start to work on those areas where you think that a little extra effort could bring about the greatest improvement.

Precision and control

Precision and control 1

Tongue twisters

Practise saying some tongue twisters out loud. As you practise, notice that you are able to get progressively faster. Work at making your diction clearer.

> You've no need to light a night-light
> On a light night like tonight,
> For a night-light's light's a slight light,
> And tonight's a night that's light.
> When a night's light, like tonight's light,
> It is really not quite right
> To light night-lights with their slight lights
> On a light night like tonight.

Betty Botter had some butter,
'But,' she said, 'this butter's bitter.
If I bake this bitter butter,
it would make my batter bitter.
But a bit of better butter–
that would make my batter better.'
So she bought a bit of butter,
better than her bitter butter,
and she baked it in her batter,
and the batter was not bitter.
So 'twas better Betty Botter
bought a bit of better butter.

> She sells sea shells by the sea shore.
> The shells she sells are surely seashells.
> So if she sells shells on the seashore,
> I'm sure she sells seashore shells.

A Tudor who tooted a flute
tried to tutor two tooters to toot.
Said the two to their tutor,
'Is it harder to toot
or to tutor two tooters to toot?'

> A flea and a fly flew up in a flue.
> Said the flea, 'Let us fly!'
> Said the fly, 'Let us flee!'

One-One was a racehorse.
Two-Two was one, too.
When One-One won one race,
Two-Two won one, too.

Precision and control 2

International tongue twisters

Dutch	Leentje leerde Lotje lopen op de lange Lindelaan. Maar omdat Lotje niet wilde lopen liet Leentje Lotje staan.
French	Un chasseur sachant chasser sait chasser sans son chien de chasse.
Finnish	Vesihiisi sihisi hississä.
German	Fischers Fritze fischt frische Fische; Frische Fische fischt Fischers Fritze.
Gujarati	Kala Kaka a Kali Kaki ne Kanma Kahyu Ke Kando Kapi Kachumber Kar.
Irish	Tá ceann tuí ar trí thigh atá thíos le taobh na toinne.
Italian	Trentatré Trentini entrarono a Trento, tutti e trentatré, trotterellando.
Norwegian	Ibsens ripsbusker og andre buskvekster.
Portuguese	Compadre compre pouca capa parda porque quem pouca capa parda compra pouca capa parda gasta. Eu pouca capa parda comprei e pouca capa parda gastei.
Spanish	Tres tristes tigres tragaban trigo en un trigal.
Swedish	Sju skönsjungande sjuksköterskor skötte sjuttiosju sjösjuka sjömän på skeppet Shanghai.
Xhosa	Iqaqa laqabaleka iqhini latyibalika laqhawula uqhoqhoqho.
Zulu	Ingqeqebulane yaqaqela uqhoqhoqho, uqhoqhoqho waqaqela iqaqa, iqaqa laqalaza.

Keep in good voice

❑ **Drink plenty of water** – dry vocal chords will prevent you from getting the best from your voice. Drink water first thing in the morning, before and during your presentation.

❑ **Limit caffeine intake** – caffeine is a diuretic and will dehydrate the throat and vocal chords. Alcohol also has a drying effect and should be avoided.

❑ **Avoid eating late at night** – this can cause acid reflux spilling into the larynx, causing hoarseness.

❑ **Avoid tensing or straining your neck.**

❑ **Avoid forcing the voice** – learn to project or use a microphone.

Section 2

Chapter 5

Dress, Etiquette and Achieving Professional Credibility

- Creating good first impressions
- Dressing for success
- Dressing tips for women
- Dressing tips for men
- Grooming and personal hygiene
- Etiquette
- Good manners
- Making introductions

- Attending a function
- Table etiquette
- Proposing a vote of thanks
- Hosting a dinner
- Looking after guests
- Choosing a menu
- Selecting wines
- Achieving credibility

Creating good first impressions

'You never get a second chance to make a first impression!'

First impressions are **VITAL** – they are powerful and often permanent.

A large part of the first impression that you give will be created by how you carry yourself, your voice and your appearance – all of which contribute to whether or not you have professional impact. We have already looked at posture, deportment and voice and this section will focus on other factors, such as your personal presentation, the clothes you have chosen to wear and whether you are comfortable socially.

Dressing for success

Dressing appropriately is all part of being 'set for success'. If possible, research your audience in advance and make sure that you conform to their cultural norms and dress code. Be aware that it is equally possible to be over-dressed, as it is to be underdressed.

Do not compromise on smartness however, and do not allow your appearance to overpower your message.

People like people who look like them, so adapt your outfit to tone in with your audience's style. Getting it right is yet one more subtle signal that you are in tune with them.

Dressing tips for women

❑ **Make sure that your clothes fit you properly** – ill-fitting (particularly tight) clothing is rarely flattering.

❑ **Dress according to your body type** – certain styles will compliment your figure, whilst others will flatter you less. If you need help in determining which styles are best for you, seek advice. (The complimentary 'personal shopper' facility available in large departmental stores is one option.)

❑ **Find a colour palette that suits you** – although there are no strict rules about who can wear which colours, you should know which colours flatter you most.

❑ **Dress tastefully** – remember that, as you are representing your company at all times, you should avoid wearing very short skirts, low-cut blouses and dresses, and sheer clothing at work.

❑ **Make sure that your underwear does not show through your clothing** – carry a spare pair of tights in case of ladders.

❑ **Pay attention to your shoes** – keep the heel of your shoes at a low or medium height and choose shoes that cover your toes. Keep your shoes polished.

❑ **Accessorise well, but in moderation** – avoid jewellery that jangles as it can become a distraction for your audience.

Dressing tips for men

❑ **Do not get into a rut and wear the same thing every day** – you can vary your look by wearing different shades and fabrics. Be careful to choose clothing that is crease resistant and will not show perspiration.

❑ **Discover which colours are flattering to you** – white shirts may be the norm, but you may look better in a subtle cream shade. The same goes for suits, which come in a wide range of neutral shades. You may be surprised at how much better you look in one shade of grey than you do in another.

❑ **Your clothing should fit you well** – do not buy something if it is too tight or baggy.

❑ **Choose jacket and trouser styles that flatter you** – it is easy to be led by fashion, but seek specialist advice from a gentlemen's outfitter – you can still buy your clothes from a chain store!

If you are thin, you might try a double-breasted jacket and flat-fronted trousers to make yourself look broader. Conversely, if you are on the heavy side, you might opt for single-breasted jackets and trousers with pleats.

Braces or a belt will help the trousers hang well and over-long trousers should always be shortened – you are unlikely to grow into them!

❑ **Select your ties carefully** – particularly when presenting, choose a tie with some red in it. It is generally safest to choose subtle colours and conservative patterns. As a rule, novelty ties are not appropriate in a business setting.

❑ **Co-ordinate your belts and shoes with your outfit** – belts and shoes should be the same colour as each other and shoes should be in good repair and polished.

❑ **If you choose to wear jewellery, make sure that it is tasteful** – flashy jewellery does not enhance your business image and will be a distraction for your audience.

Whatever you wear, the most important thing is to make sure that it is smart, practical, comfortable and helps you to feel good about yourself!

Grooming and personal hygiene

Although having appropriate clothing is very important, being clean, well groomed and well cared for is even more important.

- ❏ **Be aware of personal hygiene** – make sure you bathe or shower and apply a deodorant/antiperspirant every day.

- ❏ **Try to clean your teeth after you eat** – it is easy to carry disposable teeth wipes. If you cannot, suck on a breath mint to freshen your breath.

- ❏ **Be subtle with scents** – apply perfume, cologne, or aftershave sparingly. Bear in mind that you become accustomed to the smell, so it may be harder for you to detect on yourself than it will be for others.

- ❏ **Trim your hair regularly** – keep it looking fresh and grease-free by washing it often. Use an anti-dandruff shampoo, if you need to.

- ❏ **Pay attention to your nails** – they should be clean and neat.

Etiquette

How you behave and carry yourself in public situations is fundamentally important to the image that you present. There are bands of appropriate behaviour, ranging from the very formal – which is often traditional and ritualised – to the very informal.

Companies and organisations, just like families, will have their own way of doing things – and this in turn will be tempered by the cultural norms of local geographical areas, where there may be a different approach to formality, hierarchy, dress and behaviour.

Be aware that what is acceptable in one environment may be totally unacceptable in another. A good rule of thumb is usually to follow the example offered by your host and to err on the side of caution, or conservativeness.

In other words:

> **'When in Rome, do as the Romans do.'**

You can protect yourself further by:

- ❏ being alert to the possibility of cultural differences.

- ❏ researching the company or country you are visiting in advance.

- ❏ asking for guidelines around specific events or norms from your host, or from colleagues.

Chapter 5 – Dress, Etiquette and Achieving Professional Credibility

Good manners

As a minimum, you will be expected to display the basics of good manners from your own culture and to apply them in an unobtrusive way. This is an entry qualification to being seen as being 'professional'.

You should adjust your preferences in deference to the other party, but always err on the side of good manners.

In her book, *Watching the English*, Kate Fox explains how making a simple purchase – say, buying a cup of coffee – will involve the average English person in saying 'Thank you' at least 5 times. This might be a demonstration of an innate politeness, or an over-eagerness not to be thought rude – either way, being seen as being courteous is better than not!

Making introductions

Another potential minefield is introductions – when to shake hands? When to air kiss, when not to air kiss? It is hard to make hard and fast rules, but in general it is better to err on the side of caution.

Introductions are less formal than they used to be, when the historical norm was to introduce the younger person to the older, the lower ranking to the more senior. As a host, it is always polite to check whether people know each other – and if not, to introduce them, perhaps adding some nugget of information about each one which might enable them to start conversation with one another.

When shaking hands, wait for the more senior person to offer a hand first and then respond, using a firm grip (avoid the 'limp fish') and make two or three vertical shakes, before releasing.

In a formal environment or when first being introduced, make eye contact, smile and either use the ubiquitous: 'Pleased to meet you ...', the less formal 'Hello ...', or if you think they did not catch your name, (or you want them to repeat theirs) say: 'Hello, I'm ...'. Do not allow this process to become lingering.

To display additional warmth to an acquaintance who you are happy to see, take their right hand in yours and simultaneously touch the back of their hand lightly with two fingers of your left hand, while you shake hands. A more effusive version of this is take their right hand in both of yours and shake; while a yet more familiar version is to place your left hand on their upper arm, whilst you shake hands in the normal way.

Make sure that your facial expression and what comes out of your mouth is aligned with this positive and very friendly body language and that your approach is tailored to the person and the occasion.

Greeting with an air kiss should only happen once both parties have been introduced and know each other – it is more common in Europe than the UK, but in business terms is a good signal that the relationship is moving from the formal to the less formal.

A current trend is for younger people to greet each other with a hug or a high-five, as a norm. Be aware that older and more senior people will not be as comfortable with this – give them some space!

Whether you have made an effort with your appearance – how you dress, whether your hair is tidy, whether your shoes are clean, whether you have shaved – is as important as whether you eat untidily, smoke during a meal, or answer your phone whilst conducting a meeting. In the business environment everything that you do is noticed and adds data to other people's perception of you.

If you are likely to need a business card, make sure that you carry some and that they are clean and do not look second hand. If clients are likely to have to visit your office, your desk or to travel in your car, it is imperative to ensure that they are all clean, tidy and organised.

If you apply good manners, are personally tidy and organised, you will create a strong 'first impression'. However, if you fall short in any of these areas the resultant *faux pas* could be a 'deal breaker'!

Attending a function

Always ensure that you have all of the information that you need – what is the dress code – is it a black-tie event? Check the times of the function, the full name and address of the venue and the transport options in order to avoid arriving late or in a stressed state. Have a 'back-up' contingency plan and all necessary contact telephone numbers, in case there are any problems. Also check the transport arrangements for your departure. It may be a late finish!

Table etiquette

Remember your table manners:

❑ **When ordering for yourself, be sensible and safe with your choices** – do not be over-adventurous just for the sake of it or because you are dining at someone else's expense.

❑ **Do not start too soon** – after you see the host or the guest of honour do so, place your own napkin in your lap. In 'up-market' restaurants, the waiter will do this for you.

❑ **The host should indicate to invite the guest(s) of honour to begin eating** – following which everyone may commence their meals.

❑ **Cutlery will have been laid at your place setting according to the menu and foods that you ordered** – start from the outer utensils and progress inwards with each course. Drinks should always be placed to the right above your place setting, and condiments and accompaniments such as bread to the left.

Never pick up dropped cutlery. Tell a member of the serving staff that you have dropped an item of cutlery – they will then pick it up for you and bring a replacement.

❑ **During the meal** – do not bend over your food whilst eating and avoid propping your elbows on the table, although it is acceptable to rest your hands or forearms on the edge.

❑ **If you have a problem** – either with an external issue or regarding the meal, always speak quietly with a member of staff. Should it be necessary to leave the room or the table, do so unobtrusively, excusing yourself as you do so.

❑ **At the end of the meal** – as you leave the table, place your napkin to the left of your plate.

❑ **Do not put handbags or mobile phones** (which should be switched off) **on the table** – should it be necessary to have a phone activated, leave it in silent mode and leave the table to take, or make, any urgent call.

❑ **As a guest, do not over-indulge in alcohol** – just because it is there and you are not paying for it, never drink excessively or act aggressively. The behaviour of a guest should always be 'polite and proper'.

Remember that people will be making judgements based on the way that you handle yourself in social situations and while dining.

Proposing a vote of thanks

On occasions, you may be asked to make a spontaneous 'thank you' speech, or to offer a vote of thanks. This will probably reflect on the fact that you are seen as being a 'good speaker' and you should remember that you are speaking on behalf of the whole audience.

Stick with the Four Corner-stones (particularly the first three: Purpose, Audience and Content). Be clear about what you have been asked to deliver; tune into what the audience will expect you to say on their behalf and draw together some bullet point content.

Apply the technique of the X-ray Sheet. Jot down what you want to say by way of introduction; find a grab and list your key points. Look for an opportunity to highlight your content (tell a relevant story or anecdote) and close with a 'call to arms', inviting the audience to join with you in thanking (applauding) person A, B or C, or by proposing a toast.

Hosting a dinner

Looking after guests

If you are the host, the priority is for you and your guests to feel comfortable with their surroundings and company.

Make sure that you have provided all the information that your guests will need to find the venue and to understand the parameters of the event and that you have all the information that you will need to make introductions.

When arranging seating, it is the norm to alternate the male and female diners, at the same time basing your plan on the individual seniority, responsibilities, background and interests of your party members.

Choosing a menu

❑ **The location of your venue may mean that it is a good opportunity to try local specialities** – perhaps seafood or regional dishes. Make sure that you know how to eat your chosen food before you order, for example it can be difficult to tackle crabs claws whilst talking with a client!

❑ **If you need to select a menu for guests, be aware of possible dietary and ethnic considerations.** If possible research your guests' preferences in advance to ensure that they will be comfortable with your choices, otherwise be sure to check with them before you finalise the order.

As a host, do ensure that there is an adequate supply of the wines available for your guests and always provide mineral or tap water. Also ensure that a range of non-alcoholic drinks are available for drivers, or non-drinkers.

Selecting wines

When choosing your wines, the only 'rule' is that they should perfectly match and compliment the foods that you or your guests are eating. Traditionally red wines have accompanied meat dishes, and whites, fish dishes – but this is now no longer the case.

It is the weight, (or body) and flavour of the wines that is important. Light foods should be accompanied by a light wine, whilst heavy foods are best accompanied by heavier wines.

Order and choose with confidence; as with your food choices – if in doubt play safe, and ask advice as to possible recommendations from knowledgeable staff at the venue.

A 75cl. bottle of wine serves 4-5 standard glasses of wine. Always ensure that you have requested an adequate number of bottles for your number of guests.

When ordering a bottle of wine, the waiter will bring it to the table for you to inspect. Check that the correct wine has been brought and that the bottle's external appearance does not show any damage or leakage. Should this occur, politely decline the bottle and request a replacement.

It is important that all wines are served at the correct temperature. White wines should be served cool, not over cold and red wines should be served at room temperature.

The waiter will remove the cork in front of you and the guests. You will be offered a small amount of the wine to 'taste'. Gently swirl it in the glass to check its colour and clarity, and to inhale the aroma. If necessary, the wine can also be sipped to confirm that it is in good condition.

Any faulty wine should again be discreetly reported to the waiter and a replacement provided.

A faulty wine will always smell faulty. Do not be afraid to reject a wine if it smells 'off' to you. If it smells off – it is!

Once checked, the waiter will pour wine for all the guests, starting with any ladies present and returning lastly to the host. Every bottle opened should be checked in this same way, and glasses never topped up from a new bottle without being checked.

Consider offering after-dinner drinks too: port to accompany cheese; brandy, whisky or liqueurs with coffee.

If you or a guest has a request or complaint relating to the meal, discreetly attract the attention of the relevant member of staff. Never shout across the room or table, and definitely no finger clicking!

Should a guest be unwell, always ensure that he or she is accompanied if leaving the room and provided with any necessary care and attention.

If hosting with colleagues, it may be useful to nominate different roles, so that there is always someone giving attention to each aspect of the occasion.

At the end of the event, ensure that your guests are able to get home safely – this may mean that you have to imbibe less than everyone else!

Etiquette rules have developed over centuries and are useful as a guide. Always be conscious of religious, cultural and regional norms and the impact that they have upon behaviour and the selection of food and drink.

Behaving 'properly' need not be a straitjacket. Getting it right will contribute to your gravitas and enable you to achieve professional impact. Use these guidelines as a steer – be yourself – but also remember:

'Manners maketh man.'

Motto of Winchester College and New College, Oxford
William of Wykeham, (1324 – 1404)

Achieving credibility

Section 1 introduced the Four Corner-stones and the X-ray Sheet – the first of four strands – which guarantee good, well-structured content.

Section 2 has focused on you and the way that you come across to others. This content has created a virtuous circle in which aligning your body, your mind and considering the way that you present yourself to others, have positioned you to be able to deliver your fantastic content with enhanced credibility.

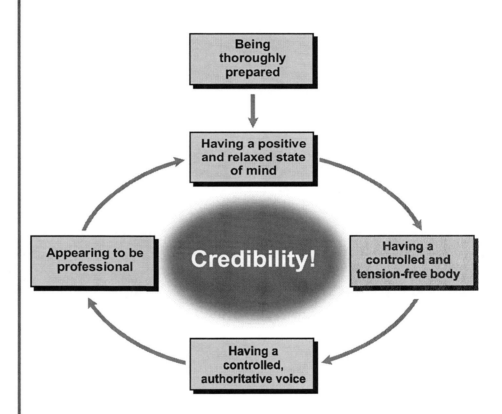

Sections 3 and 4 will ensure that you have considered the remaining variables which, if you get them right, will mean that you will also be able to deliver with impact!

Section 3

Chapter 6

Engaging with Your Audience

- Appealing presenters

- Achieving rapport with your audience

- Tactics

- Eye contact

- Using appropriate language

- Using metaphors, analogies and stories

- Adjusting your style to suit the group size

Appealing presenters

Have you ever attended a presentation where you felt you could not relate to the speaker? Why was that?

_____

_____

_____

_____

What other possible reasons might there be for presenters to lack engagement?

_____

_____

_____

_____

Who are your favourite public speakers? Why do you warm to them particularly? What is it about the way that they present themselves that appeals to you?

_____

_____

_____

_____

Are there any aspects of the things that they do well that you could implement or develop in your own presentations?

_____

_____

_____

_____

Achieving rapport with your audience

There is a good chance that the speakers you like manage to engage with you and achieve some level of rapport, whilst those you like less, do not.

Some people have a real skill for building rapport and they have the ability to make the people around them feel that they are 'in tune' or 'on the same wavelength'. Often their listeners talk about these people as being 'in step', 'a kindred spirit' or as being 'one of us' – and if that is the case, it probably does not happen by chance!

Many people know the saying:

'I hear and I forget, I see and I remember, I do and I understand.'

Those people who really understand about rapport would probably add:

'Involve me and I am certain.'

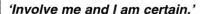

In presentation terms, rapport is really about conveying to the listener the feeling that they are somehow being 'engaged' in the event and are part of the discussion, which is interesting and relevant to them.

To achieve this, presenters have to want to bother to put themselves out and to work to make their material of interest. Some presenters, who are not prepared to take this step, blame the audience when things do not go as well as they would have liked – but there are no bad audiences – just bad presenters!

It is really important for a presenter to understand: if you can establish rapport with your audience then they will be on your side, contributing to making the event a success. Without rapport, they will feel that your presentation is something which is 'happening to them', which at best will just wash over them, but at worst, will be something that they feel they have to endure.

Remember: You are never alone when you make a presentation, but without rapport it will feel that way!

Presenters who do not attempt to establish rapport are making life very hard for themselves. Successful presentations are normally inclusive affairs, where the presenters have made clear that they value their listeners' experience and have respect for their time.

You can increase involvement during your presentation by encouraging feedback. Look for ways to develop rapport with your audience and give them opportunities to respond.

Tactics

Getting the audience to respond:

- ❑ **Ask questions** – open-ended questions draw out ideas, opinions and experiences, whilst closed questions are good for checking understanding.

- ❑ **Use rhetorical questions** – these will prompt interest and response from the audience without there being any interruption to the presentation.

- ❑ **Use humour** – you do not need to tell a joke, but instead look for moments of spontaneous humour. Allow your natural warmth to show through. People will not expect you to be 'funny', but they would like you to be 'fun'.

- ❑ **Personalise your presentations** – use names, 'buzz words', local knowledge or shared experiences.

- ❑ **Include anecdotes** – people are curious, and love stories, but they must be appropriate to the presentation and to the listeners.

- ❑ **Make your presentation 'human'** – this will help the audience to relate to you and your message.

- ❑ **Project enthusiasm and sincerity** – not least because it is infectious!

Remember: you will need to allow the audience time to respond to you and you must respond to them. Always acknowledge their contributions – laugh at their jokes – even if you have heard them a hundred times before.

Eye contact

It is very important to give appropriate eye contact, because it is a fundamental in developing rapport, and using it well shows that you are:

- ❑ confident
- ❑ sincere
- ❑ honest
- ❑ interested in your audience.

and, it gives you the opportunity to 'read' the audience and to respond to them accordingly.

Common errors:

- ❑ **Eye contact can sometimes be lost to notes, visuals, the ceiling, the floor or to the windows** – at best, you will appear to be nervous and at worst your body language will be interpreted as suggesting that any of these things are more interesting to you than the audience is!
- ❑ **Focusing on the friendly face** – the rest of the audience will feel ignored and can easily become restless.
- ❑ **Unconvincing 'search light' sweeps, mechanical, or fleeting eye contact** – these can appear insincere and so are less likely to gain a response. Individuals must know that they are getting eye contact.
- ❑ **Frequent changes** – make you appear shifty, and suggest that you are holding back information.

Positive strategies:

- ❑ **Establish eye contact immediately** – 'hit' as many individuals as possible, even before you begin to talk.
- ❑ **Pay attention to everyone in your audience** – this makes it much more likely that they will pay attention to you.
- ❑ **Combine strong eye contact with some other supporting gesture** – a smile or a nod will help to make it even more convincing.
- ❑ **Keep eye contact random**.
- ❑ **Cover the whole audience** – in larger groups, you can achieve this by 'hitting' blocks of people.

Practise giving about 4 to 5 seconds of eye contact to each individual.

Using appropriate language	It is possible to completely alienate an audience by using inappropriate language and the key is to make your language accessible.

❑ **Use conversational speech** – this is easy to understand. Avoid 'bad' language (swearing or blaspheming) and try not to use colloquialisms.

❑ **Avoid jargon, TLAs (three-letter acronyms!) and technical terms** – these can easily make people feel excluded. They should not be used unless you know that the audience is familiar with them, in which case they **may** be used in an inclusive way and to your advantage.

❑ **Use a pause** – eliminate any non-words or personal 'catch-phrases' that may become distracting.

❑ **Distinguish between written and spoken language** – the audience need to feel that they are listening to an interesting person, rather than being read a script.

❑ **Keep the main point of the sentence near the beginning** – this means that the audience will understand where you are taking them and will be able to follow your thread.

❑ **Use active rather than passive verbs** – for example: 'Seat belts **save** lives', rather than: 'Lives are saved by using seat belts'.

❑ **Never say not!** – humans think best in positives, rather than negatives. Leave out anything that is likely to confuse, e.g. 'I'm not here to sell you anything'.

❑ **'Signpost' your presentation** – let people know that you are finishing a key point by summarising it and flag-up each fresh point or new section clearly.

❑ **Use examples, case studies, stories and analogies** – to support and add value to your case. |
| **Using metaphors, analogies and stories** | Trying to explain a complex point, or a technical idea can sometimes be extremely difficult. One way to bring everyone to the same level of understanding and explain what you mean more easily is to use analogies, metaphors or stories. |
| **Analogy example 1** | This technique could be used in helping us to understand the enormity of figures.

Saying that: *'The National Debt has increased by £1 billion'* does not mean very much to most people – it is hard to visualise and comprehend.

By using an analogy and saying that: *'1 million seconds amounts to 11 days'* and that *'1 billion seconds therefore is equal to 4 months'*, we can get more of a 'feel' for the information. |

Analogy example 2

This is how Greenpeace successfully used an analogy to explain the challenge facing our World.

'The Earth is 4,600 million years old, and this is what has happened to it.

If we condense this inconceivable time span into an understandable concept, we can liken the Earth to a person of 46 years of age.

Nothing is known of the first 7 years of this person's life, and whilst only scattered information exists about the middle span, we know that only at the age of 42 did the Earth begin to flower.

Dinosaurs and the great reptiles did not appear until one year ago, when the planet was 45. Mammals arrived only 8 months ago: in the middle of last week man-like apes evolved into ape-like men, and at the end of last weekend the ice age enveloped the Earth. Modern man has been around for 4 hours.

During the last hour, Man discovered Agriculture.

The industrial revolution began one minute ago.

During those sixty seconds of biological time, Modern Man has made a rubbish tip of Paradise.'

Metaphor examples

In his book *'A Whack on the Side of the Head'*, Roger von Oech gives examples of metaphors for 'The Meaning of Life'. He says:

'Life is like a bagel. It's delicious when it's fresh and warm, but often it's just hard. The hole in the middle is its great mystery, and yet it wouldn't be a bagel without it.'

'Life is like a jigsaw puzzle, but you don't have the picture on the front of the box to know what it's supposed to look like. Sometimes, you're not even sure if you have all the pieces.'

'Life is like a room full of open doors that close as you get older.'

Story example 1

On our Time Management workshops, we sometimes tell and act out the story of packing the boot of our car for a family holiday.

The story lends itself to play-acting, drama, mime and a degree of pathos, but the purpose for telling it is to create a memorable image that carries a fundamentally important point. We want people to truly understand that they should pack their day in the same way that intelligent people going on holiday would pack the boot of a car – by putting the big things (suitcases) in first and using the little things to fill the gaps around the edges.

In Time Management, this is a simple but fundamentally important point, and so is worthy of added effort to highlight it.

Story example 2

We once used a different story with a mining company in Sweden to make the same point. This involved relating how a trainer demonstrated the 'boot packing theory' by using a container, some rocks (representing big tasks), some pea-shingle (representing medium-sized tasks) and some sand (representing small 'to-do' list type tasks).

In the story, the trainer filled the container with sand (representing small 'to-do' list type tasks) first and (what a surprise) had no room for medium or big tasks (shingle or rocks) – the important things!

So he began again. This time, he put the rocks into the container first and although it was in theory 'full', still managed to get some pea-shingle and sand into the gaps. Again, this picture story was intended to demonstrate the theory of putting the big tasks in first and using the other tasks for what they are – great gap-fillers!

Looking at the audience with satisfaction, the trainer then realised that one audience member had something that they wanted to add.

Holding great eye contact with the trainer, he said:

'Do you know what – at this stage you should reach down to your briefcase and pull out a bottle of cold Carlsberg. Take the lid off and slowly pour it into the container – I bet none will overflow – and then you could say to the audience:

… and no matter how full your day, there's always some space left for a beer!'

If you use a story, make sure that it is relevant and works, adapting the content to suit each audience.

Never worry about being upstaged by the audience – if they make the joke, they will enjoy it all the more and will be even more likely to remember your message!

Adjusting to suit the group size

Generally, a smaller audience will provide more opportunity for the presentation to be informal, conversational and interactive – whilst with a larger audience, it is more appropriate to 'present' and then to take questions.

Small audience – a group of 12 or less
Informal	Formal
Application	**Application**
• This is ideal for coaching and training events and for presenting new ideas or making a sale to an established customer.	• This is ideal for committee meetings, sales pitches to new clients and presentations to senior groups.
Techniques	**Techniques**
• Welcome the audience individually.	• Adhere to corporate culture and norms.
• Use informality to break the ice.	• Wear formal business clothing and follow more formal procedures.
• Grab and involve the audience quickly.	• Establish eye contact with each member of the group quickly.
• Let them know that you are driving the event, but that their contributions are welcome.	• Demonstrate to them that you are structured and well prepared.

Large audience – a group of 13 or more
Informal	Formal
Application	**Application**
• This is ideal for 'spontaneous' presentations at a more formal company-wide or conference style event.	• This is ideal for structured and pre-planned inputs at shareholders meetings, large public events or company-wide conferences.
Techniques	**Techniques**
• Rehearse your informality.	• Adhere to corporate culture and norms, but allow your personality to shine through.
• Move away from a fixed podium and towards the audience.	• Wear formal business clothing.
• Create a virtue out of making a break from rigid structure.	• Keep things formal and correct and use humour with care.
• Use humour, but keep the content general, simple, relevant and to the point.	• Link, summarise, emphasise and repeat your key points.

You may not have a choice about the audience size – but you will have an opportunity to decide how to respond to it! Give thought to the size of the audience and always adjust your presentation accordingly.

Section 3

Chapter 7

Making It Memorable

- Memorable presentations

- The attention curve

- Primacy, recency and frequency

- Ways to highlight and lift attention

- Inhibitors to retention

- Your personal energy

Memorable presentation

Consider the best presentations that you have ever attended. What made them so memorable?

_____

_____

_____

_____

_____

_____

_____

What can you learn from this?

_____

_____

_____

_____

It is of course essential that your presentation is memorable for the right reasons!

No matter how good you or your content is, people's attention will inevitably ebb and flow.

You should be aware that many people work hard to get to an event, and when they arrive, it is with a sense of relief: 'Phew, made it …'

If you observe these people closely, it will become apparent that only their bodies have actually arrived – their brains are still on their journey, back at their desk or thinking about some things that they really should have done before rushing out!

You will need to get these people's attention with a good 'grab' early on, to make them sit up, focus on you and give their full attention to your message.

Once you have started, people's attention will still come and go. It is worthwhile understanding that they will remember the information received at the high points on their attention curve most readily – and so you should plan the flow of your presentation to take full advantage of this!

The attention curve

The attention curve of a 'basic' presentation is likely to be similar to that shown below, with the audience being most easily 'tuned in' at the beginning and at the end.

Primacy, recency and frequency

In general, people find it easiest to remember:

☐ things that happened first or last

☐ things which are repeated

☐ things which are in some way very ***distinctive***.

For this reason, it is up to the presenter to highlight key points and to raise the attention levels of the listener. The more peaks of attention that are proactively created for the audience, the more they will remember.

Greater variety = greater impact = greater retention

From any presentation the listener can be expected to retain around 5% of any new information – it is essential to ensure that it is the key 5%!

This is the content that should be highlighted in blue on the X-ray Sheet (see Chapter 1).

Ways to highlight and lift attention

There are innumerable ways to highlight key points and lift attention. Use the list below as a prompt – find the right tactic to suit your situation.

❑ **Use your voice** – alter the pace, pitch, volume. Remember to pause.

❑ **Movement and gestures** – look for opportunity to move with purpose. Find ways to use movement and gestures to create a pictorial image and add value to your message. Be careful to maintain a balance between too much and too little movement.

❑ **Personalise** – use people's names, focused examples and language that they can relate to.

❑ **Praise and recognition** – include positive examples of successes from peoples own experiences. Ask people to give examples. Encourage them, recognise them and thank them for their contributions.

❑ **Quizzes and competitions** – are fun and very motivational for some people. They are also a great aid to retention and will enable you to check understanding. Most important of all, they provide an opportunity to give prizes!

❑ **Analogies, metaphors and examples** – use analogies to simplify complex ideas and bring everyone to the same level of understanding (see Chapter 6).

❑ **Anecdotes and stories** – everyone loves a story, but they must be appropriate and focused. Never leave the audience thinking 'So what?' Always use anecdotes and stories that are inclusive and to which your audience will be able to relate.

❑ **Humour** – humour is good, but needs to be handled carefully. Before including it, ask yourself:

• Will people understand it (as I intend it)?
• Will they find it funny?

Be wary of international audiences – humour can be very regional and like wine, does not always travel!

❑ **Grabs and props** – can really help people to sit up and take notice and like analogies and stories can help to crystallise their understanding.

- ❏ **Handouts** – provide a great way to summarise at one extreme and to pass out additional data and information, at the other.

- ❏ **Repetition** – nothing beats hearing the same point from a different direction. If you want people to remember it, tell them, tell them, tell them.

- ❏ **Quotations** – a well chosen quotation can have incredible impact. It allows a presenter to align themselves with an idea of substance, or words of wisdom from a great individual, who already has credibility and standing in this area.

- ❏ **The 'rule of three'** – the brain handles clusters of three very well. You can count them off on your fingers and if the words have been crafted, the rhythm of delivery is likely to be good. Using alliteration (Big, Bold and Beautiful), will also help people to tune in and remember – but do not over do it!

- ❏ **Mnemonics** – can really help people to remember – especially if they are funny, or relevant. Surely we all remember: 'Every Good Boy Deserves Food' from music lessons at school.

- ❏ **Questions** – use questions to let the audience know that you want to encourage two-way communication. A question demands a response, even if it is only a nod of the head.

- ❏ **Change the presentation style** – for example, move into a workshop or brainstorming session.

- ❏ **Vary the input** – use different speakers or introduce 'expert' interventions to add stimulus.

- ❏ **Use an activity, icebreakers and so on** – and always endeavour to make them relevant to the learning and not just 'fun'.

- ❏ **Change the environment** – think about the lighting and perhaps use music. Be aware of the seating – the brain can only absorb as much as the backside will endure!!

- ❏ **Breaks** – people absorb and retain the things they hear first (primacy) and last (recency). Breaks will automatically double the primacy and recency peaks and fresh air, bio breaks, a stretch, a drink will all be gratefully received.

- ❏ **Visuals** – support your key points with visuals and summary slides. Make sure they are focused, distinctive and clear. Leave them on display to reinforce your message.

- ❏ **Use video, DVD and computer simulations.**

Utilising some of these ideas will help your audience to stay with you on your journey and will greatly increase the likelihood of their remembering your presentation and your key 5%. For this reason, always look for an opportunity to add some 'magic' that will distinguish you and your presentation from the norm.

Inhibitors to retention

By the same token, you should give consideration to anything which could distract your audience, or inhibit their ability to retain your key points.

What are the things that could happen during your presentation that are most likely to interrupt your flow, or deflect attention from the message that you want to convey?

_____

_____

_____

How could you prepare for these in advance (either to prevent them from happening or to deal with them when they occur)?

_____

_____

_____

Your personal energy

Often to make a presentation a success, you will need to make a conscious decision to inject energy. You may find it easier to do this at certain times or in certain circumstances than in others.

Do you find that your energy fluctuates during a day, or during the course of a week? When is your energy highest? When are you at your best?

_____

_____

_____

Have you noticed that your energy is affected by what you eat and drink? By how much rest or exercise you have taken? By how enthused you are by the task ahead?

What can you do to position yourself to be able to give of your best?

_____

_____

_____

Could you use this information to help you decide when you would be most personally energised to give a presentation?

For example, if your energy is higher early in the day, or early in the week and you have an important presentation to deliver and you are asked when you are available, it might be smart to choose one time slot above another.

When would be your prime time for presenting?

_____

_____

_____

If nothing else, most presenters recognise that both their and the audience's energy levels are likely to be low after lunch and so either avoid presenting in this slot, choose content that will suit the audience, or make sure that they have sufficient personal energy to 'feed' the audience.

As ever, awareness and having thought through a strategy can help you to overcome what might otherwise be a very difficult set of circumstances!

Section 3

Chapter 8

Using Visual Aids
and Audio Visual Equipment

- Great visuals

- Why use visual aids?

- Rules for using visual aids

- Handouts; Flipcharts; Projectors; Interactive Whiteboards; TV, Video and DVD; Sound; Music; Lectern; AutoCue

- PowerPoint and Questionnaire

- PowerPoint guidelines

- Navigating your Slide Show

- Remote controls

- Features of PowerPoint

- Technical tips for PC or laptop

- Video conferencing

- Producer

- Presenting to camera

- Audio conferencing

- Live meeting

Great visuals

When you have attended presentations previously, what were the supporting visuals that had most impact upon you?

_____

_____

_____

_____

_____

_____

What was it that made them distinctive?

_____

_____

_____

_____

Why use visual aids?

People tend to remember an event when they can 'picture it' and often they will remember the 'feel' of an event, long after they have forgotten the actual content. For this reason, it is important to give careful thought to the added value of your supporting visuals.

In our earlier chapters, we have emphasised that we believe that you are your own best visual – you can create memorable images by using gestures and movement and by building a picture through descriptive language. However, there is no doubt that considerable additional benefit can be gained from using other supporting visual aids, outlined in the following pages.

The use of visual aids to support your verbal message will add emphasis and impact to your major points. For this reason, visuals should always be linked to the key 5% of your information.

'I hear and I forget,
I see and I remember ...'
Anon

A visual must be both necessary and visual.

Before using any visual aids, always ask yourself:

❑   **What value will this visual add?**

❑   **Could I manage without it?**

If it does not add value, do not use it! Words alone are not visuals.

Ask yourself:

❑   **What will this image <u>show</u>, rather than what will this visual <u>say</u>?**

Decide what single point you most want the audience to take away with them and then produce a visual to illustrate it. Do not be tempted to hide behind visuals – they are a support, not an end in themselves.

If a picture paints a thousand words ... a simple visual can often 'capture the moment' more clearly than a string of words – letting the audience hold it in their mind's eye and putting a message across much more succinctly and memorably than words alone could ever do.

When communicating factual information, charts are easier to take in than raw statistics, and flowcharts are easier to understand than written procedures. Of course, you have an option to pass on the more detailed information to your audience in the form of an 'added value' handout, but if you think that the audience might ask for more detail, it would be sensible to have some pre-prepared supplementary slides in your PowerPoint deck.

Visuals have the advantage over text of being able to cross language and cultural boundaries – providing an opportunity to add colour and humour, as well as clarity.

Different cultures will also have differing expectations as to what a 'presentation' entails: in the UK and Europe, audiences are perfectly happy if there is little or no PowerPoint, making a presentation very presenter-centric.

In the United States however, audiences would expect a presentation to be fully supported by PowerPoint and would happily accept slides which are loaded with information. They would expect to see the agenda early and then, if the meeting was not for them, are quite likely to say so and leave – which is less likely to happen in Europe. In addition, an American audience would expect to be able to drill down to detail and to view supplementary slides, where necessary. Failure to match this expectation will damage credibility and be seen as a lack of preparation.

In Japan however, it would be a mistake to begin a presentation by showing an agenda and fixed timings – which both Europeans and Americans like. The Japanese would see this as being presumptive and rude – how can you know the agenda, unless there has been group discussion and a consensus reached?

As we have discussed elsewhere in *Stand & Deliver*, knowing your audience and adapting to cultural norms are essential pre-requisites for delivering a successful presentation!

When you run through your presentation out loud, look for opportunity to use visuals to describe an idea or concept. Use bullets to support key points and tables and graphs to clarify complex data. Look for every opportunity to use a visual to add value and illustrate your point.

Before we look at specific media, it would be useful to outline some basic rules that apply to all visuals.

Rules for using visual aids

❑ **Position visuals where everyone can see them** – to have value, visuals must be clear and large enough to be read by the entire audience.

❑ **Use pictures, graphs and diagrams wherever possible** – this will avoid a mass of text or long columns of figures.

❑ **Keep them simple** – use several visuals, or a visual that builds, rather than one complex one.

... PRESENTATIONS COME TO LIFE!

- ❑ **Use colour to help emphasis** – colours speak their own language. You might use black for bold titles, red for focus, green for positives and for provoking thought, blue for calm and power and purple for fantasy.

- ❑ **Always ask someone else to check all of your visuals** – for effect, spellings and any grammatical errors.

- ❑ **Pause when you show a visual** – the audience needs time to take it in.

- ❑ **Face and address the audience** – it is easy to be drawn into the screen or flipchart when you reveal it. This limits your eye contact and makes it more difficult for the audience to hear you.

- ❑ **Have a strategy for referring back to visuals previously used** – being able to revisit visuals, shows that you are in control of your presentation, and your key 5%.

- ❑ **Blank out visuals** – when a visual is no longer relevant to your current point, blank it out, so that you can refocus the audience's attention on you and your message.

Allow time for handling visuals – (especially build-up flipcharts and PowerPoint).

Let us now look at some different types of visual aids in greater depth.

Handouts

Handouts are always a distraction, but they can be used in a positive way to vary the dynamics, or start a discussion.

- ❑ **Let the audience know if you are going to give out handouts** – they can then decide whether or not to make their own notes.

- ❑ **Have sufficient handouts for everyone.**

- ❑ **Use pictures wherever possible** – they break up the text and add impact.

- ❑ **Put your name and contact details on to your handouts** – it is a good opportunity to keep your profile high.

Printing handouts of your PowerPoint slides

There are two different ways to print out handouts in PowerPoint 2007. Experiment with the following options to find a format that best suits your message and your audience.

Click on the **Printer icon** and click **Print what**. Select either **Handouts** or **Notes Pages**.

1. **Print Handouts option** – will give you the choice of having 1, 2, 3, 4, 6 or 9 slides printed on each page. Selecting 3 slides to a page is the most effective choice, as blank lines are printed beside each slide onto which the audience can write their own notes.

2. **Print Notes option** – will print each of your slides, one per page, with any notes that you have written shown underneath each one. Delegates have space to add further comments of their own, beneath yours.

It is possible to customise both your note and handout pages by working with their Masters. Click on the View tab and then click on the Master that you wish to edit (see Figure 1).

Figure 1

Flipcharts

It is tempting to write flipcharts off as being 'old-fashioned' or 'low-tech'. However, they are a fantastic tool which offers many benefits. They are versatile, interactive, quick to prepare, independent of electricity, inexpensive and require little expertise to use effectively. Possibly their greatest benefit is that they are a simple way to make what would otherwise be a static and formulaic presentation come to life by adding the possibility of audience participation and spontaneous use of models and diagrams.

- ❑ **Use two flipcharts if possible** – this will allow you to draw comparisons, for example to contrast positive and negative messages; or you can keep your agenda displayed on one flipchart most of the time and use the other for spontaneous ideas. Having two flipcharts will also give you a reason to move with purpose between them.

- ❑ **Prepare a 'Welcome' flipchart** – place it by the entrance to your room.

- ❑ **Stand to the side whilst writing** – if you are right-handed stand with the flipchart on your left as you face the audience (and on your right if you are left-handed). This will make it easier to maintain eye contact with the audience, ensuring that they can hear you and see your facial expression.

❑ **Use the flipcharts to pose questions or to capture ideas and suggestions from the audience** – you can prepare pages beforehand, with titles, questions or key points.

❑ **Use the audience's words and phrases** – when taking points from the audience to add to a flipchart, use their words or ask their permission to change them. Always thank people for their comments in order to encourage more contributions.

❑ **Use bright, complementary colours** – black and blue are most visible, with red best as an accent colour. Try to use thick nibbed pens, as they stand out and are easier to read.

❑ **Write clearly, using big and bold script** – if your writing is not always clear, use capitals or prepare some finished text on flipcharts in advance.

❑ **Write carefully** – this adds credibility to what you are writing. Perhaps use lined or squared flipchart paper to keep your writing level.

❑ **Leave a blank sheet in between each used sheet** – this prevents your writing showing through.

❑ **Keep silent whilst writing** – this keeps the audience's attention on the flipchart and not on what you are saying.

❑ **Use the 'dot-to-dot technique'** – pre-prepare apparently blank sheets using feint pencil as guidelines for drawing, as an aide memoir of the points you want to be sure that you make, or to ensure correct spellings.

❑ **Turn over each page once the contents are no longer relevant** – this maintains focus on you and your current point.

❑ **Have a strategy for referring to individual pages** – to locate a specific page easily, turn up the lower corner of the required pages or mark them with Post-Its, which you can then sequence.

❑ **Create expanding displays and personalise a work area** – tear off pages and stick them up on the wall to create displays. Unless you have the sort of flipchart paper that has a sticky strip on the back, you will need to use blue sticky, masking tape or tacks to mount them.

Check that you have enough paper for your session in advance and try to store it flat.

Projectors

Film, slide, OHP and data projectors

Check all equipment before the start of your presentation, and be prepared for any technical failure.

❑ **Ensure that you have a spare bulb** – and that you know how to change it!

❑ **If you have to bring equipment in from a cold environment to a warm room** – do it with time to spare (at least an hour) or condensation may build up and prevent you from being able to use it. Similarly, at the end of the presentation, do not move the projector until it has had time to cool down, or you may damage the bulb – by far the most expensive component.

❑ **Make sure that the projector is powerful enough to be seen from the back of the room.**

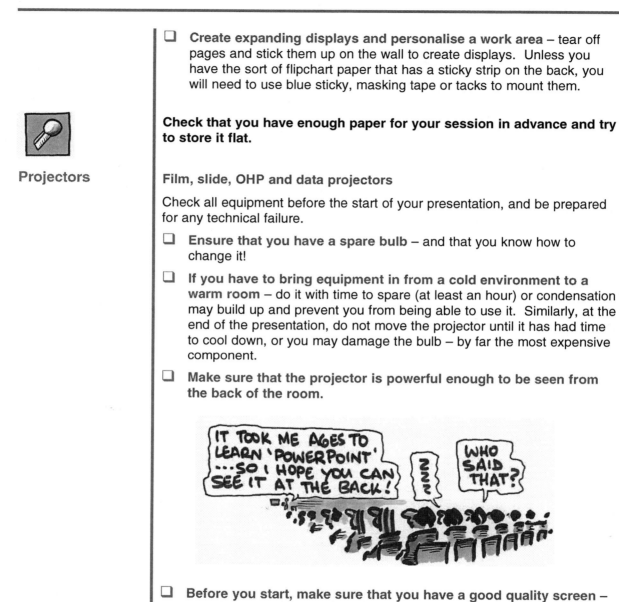

❑ **Before you start, make sure that you have a good quality screen** – which should be as large as the room will stand. Position it so that everyone can see (check lines of sight) and angle the screen forward to avoid the 'keystone' effect.

'Key-stoning' can be further addressed by adjusting the legs of the projector (unless it is ceiling mounted!) and by using the keystone controls on the projector itself.

❑ **Ensure that the slide fills the screen and check that the focus is correct.**

❑ **Address the audience rather than the screen that you are projecting on to** – do not be drawn into the large screen. As soon as you turn to the screen, your audience will find it hard to hear you and you will loose eye contact.

❑ **Keep out of the way** – position yourself where all audience members can see your visual.

❑ **Do not walk between the projector and the screen** – to avoid silhouettes or projecting onto yourself.

Be aware that in a large room, with a big audience, people further away may only be able to see the top two thirds of your screen, so you may need to plan how you fill each slide accordingly.

❑ **Blank the screen when you want to return the audience's attention to you.**

If you are operating through a PC, pressing 'B' blackens the screen and 'W' makes it go white. To return to the slide that you were on previously, press any button.

Alternatively, you can use a data projector that has an integral blank screen button. This means that you can blank the audience's screen, whilst you prepare the next slide that you wish to use on your screen. Once you have found your slide, un-blank the large screen at the projector and the audience will see what you see.

Do not blacken the projector by covering the lens with the lens cap or with paper – both are likely to make the projector overheat.

Overhead projector

As with flipcharts, it is easy to write off overhead projectors (OHPs) as being 'old-fashioned' or 'low tech' – (we agree!) and are consistently surprised by how many lecturers, trainers and speakers still use them.

Although OHPs as a delivery tool are becoming less widely used, it is now possible to make some very high quality overhead slides by colour-copying text, pictures and diagrams onto acetate. If nothing else, this may give you the feeling of having a 'safety net', should you not be able to use alternatives like PowerPoint, or if you simply want to change the stimulus and add variety.

It also means that you can write 'live' onto a slide, as you would if you had a tablet PC. This can be a great help if you are expected to reproduce and circulate outputs from your presentation, as the acetates can be easily photocopied and scanned.

❑ **If you use permanent marker to write or draw on a slide by mistake, go over it with a water-based board marker and wipe off both with a tissue** – this should leave the acetate both clean and undamaged!

❑ **Use cardboard frames for your acetates** – this will protect them and make them easier to handle. You can also write prompts or aide-memoire notes of what you plan to do or say next onto the frame itself.

❑ **Use a pointer to indicate specific information** – alternatively lay a pen (which will not roll) on to the OHP. Always point at the acetate and never turn to point at the screen.

❑ **Only switch on the projector once the transparency is in place.**

❑ **Switch the projector off as soon as possible** – this will return attention to you and your message. Always turn off before removing the visual.

❑ **Keep your acetates in organised piles** – number the frames to help you to be able to refer back or respond spontaneously to audience interaction.

Be aware that the audience is quite likely to be put off if they can see a large pile of slides – most people live in fear of 'death by slides!'

Interactive whiteboards

Linking your computer to an interactive whiteboard and a data projector will allow your images to be projected onto the whiteboard. This enables you to work on the large screen in much the same way that you would work on a tablet PC. On this occasion however, the transmitted image is controlled by touching or writing on the whiteboard with the pen provided, in addition to your being able to use a mouse or keyboard.

Benefits – using an interactive whiteboard during a presentation has several benefits, because it means that you can:

❑ **present from a standing position, maintaining good eye contact with the audience**

- ❑ **create collaborative work in documents, spreadsheets, or design projects**

- ❑ **highlight and annotate key points**

- ❑ **use it as an electronic flipchart** – with all notes and diagrams being easily saved for later use.

- ❑ **edit on the screen and save any changes or additions** – as well as being able to print them off or circulate them by e-mail after the event.

- ❑ **connect to video conferencing systems.**

Drawbacks – amongst the possible drawbacks is the fact that not all interactive whiteboard packages offer the same functions, so you must check that your presentation will run on the system that you intend to use.

There is also the danger that the audience's view of the whiteboard will be obscured by the presenter writing on it – unlike a tablet PC, where the presenter may be seated, facing towards the audience and still working interactively.

TV, video and DVD | In common with all other technology, check that the system you intend to use is working in advance of when you intend to use it.

- ❑ **Clips should be current, relevant examples that you have viewed yourself** – do not be caught out! Be aware that whilst using clips can add value and variety, they can also eat your time.

- ❑ **If you are using video, fast forward the videotape in advance so that you can start at the desired point** – this will avoid a lengthy lead-in time and maintain your flow.

- ❑ **Set the colour and volume controls in advance.**

- ❑ **Use a large screen or several screens when working with larger audiences.**

Sound

Working in the open air, in a large venue or with a big audience will all require the use of a public address system.

❑ **Practise using the microphone** – you should aim to feel comfortable moving around and be accustomed to the sound of your own voice.

❑ **Test the sound system in advance** – allow for background noise and adjust the volume accordingly.

❑ **Use a cordless or clip-on microphone** – this means that you can move more freely and use the full space that is available for you to present.

❑ **Give thought to how you position clip-on microphones** – they can exaggerate unwanted noise, such as breathing, rubbing against loose clothing, or turning pages.

Never rely on the sound technician to turn off your mike – either in between presentations, or if you go to the lavatory, always remove the batteries yourself to ensure that you are not overheard by thousands of people!

Music

No matter what size the venue, well selected music played at appropriate moments in the presentation to add emphasis to key points can work effectively to set the mood and change the tempo.

❑ **Use an iPod or MP3 player** – they are easily transportable and allow you a huge selection of music. Tailor the music to your audience and consider creating play lists for different events, audiences and moods. Certainly do not rely on 'random selection' or only play your favourite tunes!

❑ **Be careful not to overuse music in a presentation** – it can annoy and distract the audience, and effects that seemed great while you were creating the presentation can become an embarrassment during delivery!

❑ Check that the venue has a performance licence.

Whenever broadcasting sound, make sure that you have good speakers – a PC or data projector, for example, will not produce a 'big' enough sound to match the quality of pictures that they can produce, and iPod speakers will not fill a large room.

Lectern

Simply because you have been given a lectern from which to present, does not mean that you have to use it!

Do not be afraid to move away from the lectern and use the space that the stage offers. This will bring you into the audience and can be really effective if you want to demonstrate that you are not ham-strung by a predetermined script and are talking with passion, or from the heart. It also indicates that you are happy to be interactive and as a result, you are more likely to get a ready response from the audience.

This demonstrates the extent to which the way that the room is set-up can affect your presentation. Even if the venue has set things out to be formal and rigid, you can achieve a completely different 'feel' by taking control of your own environment and changing it!

AutoCue

If you are presenting using AutoCue, your presentation will need to be fully scripted in advance and will require practice if you are to deliver in an engaging way.

A script is a useful tool to use on certain occasions, particularly if:

❑ **you need to 'stay on message' for legal reasons**

❑ **your words need to be translated simultaneously.**

When writing, most people construct sentences that are grammatically correct, but the ear does not care too much about this – it is much more interested in your ideas and being able to understand them.

For this reason, it is important that your script is written in language fit for the ear and not the eye.

Text should be written in simple, straightforward sentences. Keep your structure clear and logical. Write in your pauses too!

❑ **Aim to have a rehearsal with your operator** – the AutoCue is controlled by an operator, who determines the flow of the text and they should follow you. If you stop, speed up, slow down … so should they. A rehearsal will familiarise the operator with the way that you present and give them an overview of your whole presentation. This means that you will not have to read your script word for word, but can use the screen as a prompt, and the operator will still be able to follow your 'red thread', ensuring that your script is appearing, as you need it.

❑ **Be animated** – many presenters like the safety of knowing word for word what they are going to say, but the process of reading can stifle enthusiasm and passion and make them appear 'wooden', especially if they are also tied to a lectern. To counteract this, use gestures and facial expressions and the full range of your voice, so that you appear engaging, enthusiastic and natural.

❑ **Use two screens to read from** – place one screen on either side of you. This will give you a more natural appearance, as you can move your head, maintaining a better range of eye contact across the audience.

The better you know your presentation, the better the rhythm and the more natural you will look and sound.

PowerPoint

PowerPoint can be a tremendous medium to support your getting a message across. Its use has been greatly aided by the development of tablet PCs, which allow a presenter to write on his or her screen 'live', whilst making a presentation. This enables the audience to feel that whilst the presentation may have a generic root, it is being specifically tailored for them.

PowerPoint has many features which enhance the look and layout of a presentation. It can be used to build up ideas, to add attractive video, clip-art or diagrams and to add colour and emphasis.

There is a danger, however, that these multimedia effects might be over-used and even abused – resulting in a full-blown assault on all of the senses, a mishmash of colour, style, fonts, sounds and video – which simply serve to obscure, rather than to clarify the message.

No matter how the graphics are used, they must always be relevant, otherwise there is a great risk of information overload and a clouding of the key points.

Remember, words on a screen are NOT visual aids – they are merely triggers, or prompts. Slides or other graphics are there to support the presenter, not the other way round.

PowerPoint Skills Questionnaire

If you are in the early stages of learning how to use PowerPoint, refer to the PowerPoint Skills Questionnaire in Appendix 1. This will enable you to assess your current level of competence and highlight areas that you may wish to develop.

For technical input and support, use the step by step training tutorials provided by Microsoft. You will find these at www.office.microsoft.com. Select the Training home page, then scroll down to Browse Training by Product.

> The instructions given in this section are for use with PowerPoint 2007. For earlier versions of PowerPoint, refer to Appendix 3.

PowerPoint guidelines

Slide Master – it is important to use a Slide Master when creating your presentation. This will provide a consistent 'look' and 'feel' to your presentation and will guarantee uniformity of background, colour scheme, fonts, bullet points and positioning. (To access the Slide Master, click on the **View** tab.)

Avoid displaying slide numbers on your slides. Doing so suggests that your presentation has a fixed flow and must be delivered in sequence, which in turn suggests a lack of versatility. A well organised presenter will sometimes need to adapt their presentation to reflect limitations in time, or a change to the agenda. By the same token, if you advertise a predetermined sequence, but do not follow it during your presentation, some of the audience may be distracted as they are left wondering what information was left out on the 'missing' slides!

Title slide – use a slide to head up your presentation. This should contain the title of the presentation, your name and perhaps your company/the client company logo. This is also a good opportunity to include a current theme or strap-line that gives context to your presentation. (Your own company may have a pre-set or corporate standard for this.)

Using logos – many of the presentations that you will be involved in will contain your organisation's logo and perhaps an additional customer logo. Ensure that these are current and put them onto the slide master so that they are always in exactly the same position. Logos that move from one side to the other can make a presentation look disjointed, and give the impression that a particular slide was a 'graft-on' or late afterthought.

Bullet points – keep the bullet point style consistent in your presentation. Again, using the slide master will help you to do this. Consider using creative bullet point icons to add more visual impact.

Alignment – use the proper alignment tools in PowerPoint to ensure that all lists are aligned correctly, i.e. flush left or right. Avoid using the space bar to 'line up', as this is unlikely to be accurate. A badly aligned list can draw the audience's attention away from you and what you are saying. Avoid any manual changes, unless they are really necessary.

Colour – use no more than 2-3 different colours which compliment the background that you have chosen. Too many colours detract from the clarity of each slide. (Obviously, clipart and pictures are exempt from this rule!) Check that the colours that you have chosen work in live presentations, because effects that look good on a small computer screen may not translate to the presentation room screen.

PowerPoint 2007 contains a 'Theme Color' option (versions previous to 2007 called this 'Color Schemes'), which provides colour combinations that work well together. It is straightforward to adapt these schemes to suit your presentation, and perhaps to choose colours that compliment a particular theme, or organisation's logo.

Content – avoid putting too much information onto a slide. If you do have a lot of information to impart, spread it over a number of slides or build up your slide. Audiences will have difficulty in actually reading a slide that is overloaded. As a 'rule of thumb', keep bullet points to around 6-8 items and make tables as simple as possible.

Agenda – it is possible to show a 'rolling' agenda on a tab to one side or the bottom of each slide, so that the audience has a feel for how your presentation is unfolding (see Appendix 2).

Fonts – choose a font for your presentation and stick to it. You would not expect to read a book with different typefaces for each chapter and the same goes for a presentation. Ideally and as a guide, aim for all fonts to be 28 point or larger, so that text can be easily read.

Spelling – fortunately, PowerPoint has a spellchecker! (Press F7.) Ask someone else to proof read your slides for context and spelling, even if you use spellchecker.

Images – avoid using poor quality images or standard clipart, as this can make your presentation look amateur and sloppy. Images are best kept to their original size, or smaller, to avoid a 'fuzzy' appearance.

Highlighting – decide how you are going to highlight key points. Options include animating individual slides to add emphasis and using a tablet PC, so that you can draw attention to specific items by using the pen feature to underline or highlight them. Some people choose to use a laser pointer, but be aware that these show a shaking hand and can be distracting if they start to wander!

Settings – check that the screen resolution settings on your computer are congruent with your data projector, or you may find that when you project your PowerPoint image onto the screen you lose the extreme edges of your presentation. If necessary, you can adjust the resolution whilst working in Normal View – click on the **Slide Show** tab, then click on the **Use Current Resolutions** arrow to bring up a choice of screen resolutions (see Figure 2).

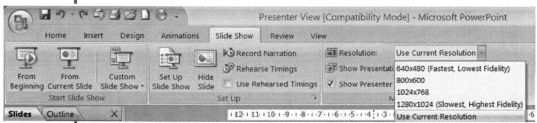

Figure 2

An alternative option is to leave a good margin around the edge of your Master Slide to avoid any mismatch.

Saving – once the PowerPoint aspect of your presentation is prepared, save it to your C-Drive, but also to a CD or Memory stick in case you need to use someone else's PC to deliver the presentation (see also Package for CD on page 112).

Navigating your Slide Show

During your presentation, you may be asked to show a slide from your PowerPoint deck out of sequence. Rather than scrolling backwards or forwards to find the right slide, you can, with some good preparation and some quick commands, find them very quickly.

Finding a slide:

❏ Once you have prepared your X-ray Sheet and PowerPoint presentation, simply write the number of each slide onto your X-ray Sheet where it will appear in your presentation. This will help you, for example when taking questions, to remember the number of a slide that was relevant to a much earlier section of your presentation.

An alternative way to find an individual slide's number is to print out a copy of your entire deck, using the print handouts option, with 9 slides to a page. (In PowerPoint, click on the **Print icon**, **Print what**, select **Handouts**, select **9 slides per page**). This provides an overview of your whole presentation – you can then manually number the slide thumbnails. This will enable you to find the required slide's number quickly and then by keying this slide number followed by return on your keyboard, the selected slide will be displayed.

The drawback with this is that you may need to revise your presentation and change the sequence of slides before the presentation is made, but after you have printed out your sheets – so you will need to remember to manually revise the numbering.

Beware – this method of jumping between slides will not work if the screen is blacked. The first touch of the button just un-blackens the screen, so typing in 21 return with a blackened screen will mean that the 2 un-blackens the screen and the 1 return will only take you to slide number 1.

❑ Alternatively work in Presenter View, where you can scroll through thumbnails of your slides on your PC and then click onto the next slide that you would like the audience to see when you are ready (see page 113 for further details).

Remote controls

There are a number of remote control devices on the market, which you can use to advance each slide. You can also use a remote mouse, or programme a mobile phone to do this for you.

The advantage – is that you are no longer physically tied to your computer and can advance or go back in your slide deck from anywhere in the room.

The drawback – is that the slides must be viewed in sequence.

Whichever method you prefer to use to navigate your slideshow, make sure that you practise and that you remain calm, in control and professional.

Features of PowerPoint

PowerPoint 2007 has many other useful features. Particularly worthy of attention are:

1. Package for CD
2. Presenter View
3. Shortcuts
4. Pen Tools

Features of previous versions of PowerPoint are explored in Appendix 3.

1. Package for CD

This feature saves your presentation, along with any linked files and associated objects – for example video clips or special fonts. It will also include the PowerPoint Viewer, which is a piece of software needed to run your presentation. Using this feature means that nothing has to be installed on a recipient's computer for the presentation to run successfully. Click on the **Microsoft icon** in the top left hand corner, select **Publish**, click **Package for CD**.

You do not have to save your presentation to a CD, but by clicking the Copy to Folder button (see Figure 3), you can save your presentation to any location that you choose and onto a memory stick if you wish.

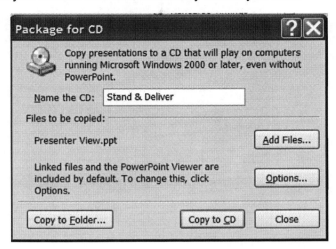

Figure 3

You can also add other presentations to the folder. For example, you may have several versions of the same presentation for different audiences. Simply click the **Add Files** button as you are creating your folder, and you can add any other files that you choose.

2. Presenter View

This feature allows you to project your full-screen slideshow to one monitor, a large screen for example, while viewing a special 'Presenter View' on another monitor, your PC for example (see Figure 4).

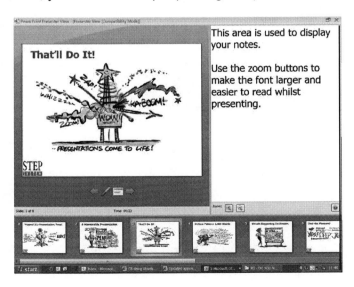

Figure 4

To set up Presenter View, open your presentation, click on the Slide Show tab and then click on the Show Presenter View box (see Figure 5). Appendix 3 outlines how to achieve this with earlier versions of PowerPoint.

Figure 5

Some advantages of using Presenter View are:

☐ **Presenter View shows thumbnails of your slides** – these are displayed along the bottom edge of your PC screen, so that you can see what is coming next. You can use these to scroll backwards or forwards to select individual slides, allowing you flexibility in the order that you deliver your content should the agenda change, or in response to a question from the audience.

☐ **A clock is displayed to show your elapsed time** – helping you to stay on track and keep control of your time.

☐ **Your notes are displayed for you** – use the zoom button to make the font a comfortable size to read whilst you are presenting. Do not rely solely on these notes. Remember that using the X-ray Sheet gives you overview of your entire presentation.

☐ **The Pointer Options icon in the centre of your screen gives access to writing and highlighting options.**

3. **Useful short cuts**

Alt and Tab buttons – there may be occasions when you need to have several applications open during your presentation, for example showing an internet site, or a product demonstration. To alternate between the different applications, hold down the Alt button, then press the Tab button. This will bring up a Task pane showing all the applications that you currently have open. You then repeatedly press the Tab button to scroll through to the application that you need. Once you release the Alt button, your computer will display the selected application.

F11 – if you are showing a web page, press F11 to remove the menu screen from the edges of the web-page. This de-clutters the edges of the visual for projection.

Shift F10 – will display a 'list of shortcuts' menu.

Ctrl P – will change the pointer to a pen. Ctrl A will revert to the pointer. Pressing E will remove any drawings made with the pen.

4. Pen Tools

Consider using a tablet PC with a write-on screen for your presentations, as this will really help to bring your presentation to life. By writing on the screen with the stylus, you can illustrate concepts spontaneously, or highlight specific points. (This feature is available on ordinary PCs too, but it takes much more practice to use a mouse to control the writing!)

During your presentation, you can access the writing features by clicking on the Pointer Options icon in the centre of your screen whilst running Presenter View. This will open a pen menu which allows you to select your pen type (Ballpoint, Felt Tip or Highlighter) and the ink colour (see Figure 6).

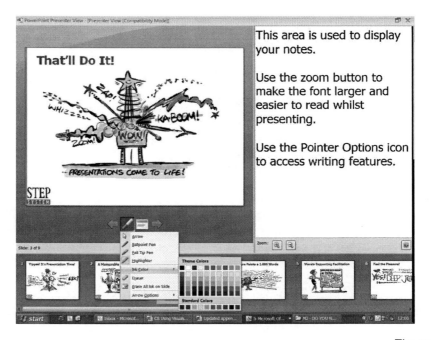

Figure 6

Any annotations that you make will stay with the slide even when you move on to a different one. If these are saved at the end of your presentation, they can form a useful record of the interaction that you have had with your audience, and is especially useful if you need to draw on that information again, or to circulate it by e-mail.

Technical tips for PC or laptop

Always make sure that the PC or laptop that you plan to use has sufficient power to deliver your presentation at an acceptable speed.

Back-up and settings:

❑ **Back up your presentation on a disc and/or memory stick** – use the Package for CD option to save your presentation (see page 112).

❑ **Run a pre-presentation check** – do not change anything once the display is working satisfactorily.

❑ **Check your screen-save options** – to avoid falling into 'hibernation' mode during your presentation.

❑ **If you need to set up your equipment in front of your audience** – have your presentation open and running, so that it is displayed as soon as you plug into the data projector.

Video conferencing

Although not strictly a presentation tool, more and more people are using video conferencing as a medium for communication. There are many proprietary and DIY set-ups available and if you are intending to use any of them, it is worthwhile looking through the guidelines for presenting to camera (see page 118).

Video conferencing certainly has some value in allowing individuals or groups to meet 'face-to-face', without their having to travel to each other – although unless you have an in-house set-up, you will need to travel to a video conferencing suite, where the equipment can be hired.

When you use this medium, think carefully about how you arrange the room and where you position the camera in relation to yourself and other colleagues. When you communicate with others through a conferencing system, notice what they do well or less well and adjust your own style and set-up accordingly in the future.

Producer

Just as conference calling has been eclipsed in many businesses by products like Live Meeting, so video conferencing is being superseded by Microsoft Producer, which lends itself rather better to presenting and training.

Producer is an add-on to PowerPoint that makes it possible to capture, synchronise and publish audio, video, slides and images. Its strength is that it can be used to create engaging and memorable presentations for training and other business communication, which can be viewed on demand in a Web browse (see Figure 7).

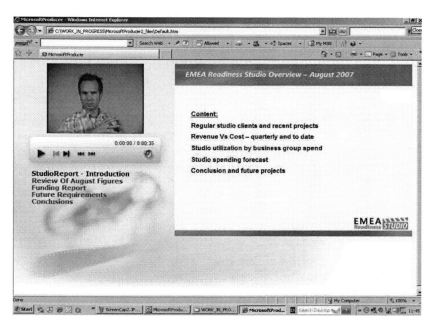

Figure 7

When it comes to making a presentation with Producer, your company's Media Specialist should be able to help you to create your video and to ensure that you are comfortable and familiar with all aspects of the production process. Always take heed of any tips that they offer and use the opportunity of their sound and other checks to practise your opening and how you will use your slides.

If you need any information about the product itself, or to access downloads, go to:

www.microsoft.com/office/powerpoint/producer/prodinfo/default.mspx.

You will also find useful tutorials at:

www.microsoft.com/office/powerpoint/producer/prodinfo/tutorials.mspx

Presenting to camera

There are several areas to consider when presenting to camera.

What to wear:

❏ **Choose plain, solid colours** – for example black, navy & cream or subdued earth tones.
- Avoid red, orange and purple, as they tend to 'bleed' at the edges.
- Avoid white, as it will drain colour from your face.
- Avoid complicated patterns, such as plaids and stripes, which can wreak havoc with the encoder.

❏ **Remove jewellery or tie pins** – these may flash and distract the viewer.

❏ **Check for stray hair** – and keep it away from your eyes.

❏ **Consider applying make-up** – it can make you look more natural and will certainly stop your face and forehead from shining.

With Producer, if you are using a Chroma-key* in your presentation, avoid wearing anything blue, or you may end up wearing the background! (*Chroma-Keying is the ability to film someone over a blue background and then replace the blue with another video or picture).

Body Language

Follow the usual body language rules and particularly the following.

❏ **Free tension in your face and shoulders.**

❏ **Look interested, focused and positive.**

❏ **Look through the camera** – as if making eye contact with an imaginary viewer. Do not allow your eyes to flick away, as this will make you appear uncertain.

❏ **Smile** – this will help you to demonstrate warmth and will cut through the lens / screen barrier.

❏ **If you are sitting, sit up and forward** – do not slump.

❏ **If you are standing, use the Ready Position** (see page 40).

If you are using Producer, ask the camera operator where the shot is – for example, on your face or face and upper body. Use gestures if your body (as far as the waist) is in shot.

Voice

- ❏ **Check your pace** – remember that being nervous is likely to cause you to speed up.

- ❏ **Speak clearly** – lift your head, so that you are not mumbling into your notes, or to the computer screen.

- ❏ **Vary your voice and let it sound natural** – inject energy and enthusiasm.

- ❏ **Have a glass of water to hand.**

and finally, when presenting to camera, remember:

- ❏ **Try to visualise your audience** – you will appear more natural and relaxed if you are talking to another human being, rather than a camera.

- ❏ **Use rhetorical questions to engage your audience** – although you cannot see the audience response, they will feel more involved.

- ❏ **If the session is to be used repeatedly** – avoid references that will date your work and which will prevent it from being suitable for any audience.

If you use PowerPoint with Producer, remember as in any presentation, slides are not your notes – the PowerPoint presentation is there to enhance your message and to add impact for the audience.

Audio conferencing

Taking part in a telephone conference call will not be viewed by many as 'making a presentation' – however, it is an opportunity to 'present yourself'.

Everyone knows that you can 'hear a smile' and by thinking about and applying your energy and managing your posture, voice and facial expression, you can ensure that you will come across at your best.

Live Meeting

Live Meeting is a hosted, real-time Web conferencing service that enables participants, (from small collaborative meetings to large-scale presentations), to communicate and collaborate with anyone, anywhere – using just a PC and an Internet connection.

Think carefully about how you use Live Meeting and, as with all of the tools outlined above, be careful, because none of them allow you to use all of your verbal and non-verbal skills as fully as you can in a face-to-face presentation. This means that any vocal or visual signals that you do give out will have increased impact and be wide open to greater misunderstanding.

Remember whilst visual aids can add value, the most important ingredient in any presentation is you!

Make the most of yourself, whenever you Stand & Deliver!

Section 4

Chapter 9

Handling Questions

- Dealing with questions
- A question is a compliment!
- Preparing for question time
- Self-preservation
- How to get the first question
- Ducking the question
- Keeping control of question time
- Question types
- Good question-handling practice
- Keeping to time
- Finishing on a positive note
- Questions in other environments
- Link expressions
- Messages

Dealing with questions

What is the worst question you have ever been asked at a presentation? How did you handle it? How could you have handled it differently?

_____

_____

_____

_____

Question time can be a challenge. There is a clear power shift as the audience moves from 'having to listen' to 'having their say'. What may have been a monologue until now, moves into being a dialogue!

Handling questions and managing question time is one of the most strategic parts of any presentation – it can make or break the whole performance.

If your view is that you want to **talk with** an audience and not **to** them – then you will recognise question time for what is – a fantastic opportunity to change gear! It is another chance to engage with the audience and include them in your presentation.

If they have questions, it is because they are interested. They may be looking for greater clarity, or for more detail; they may have an observation to make. Whatever their intention, it is up to you to manage the process and ensure that everyone takes value from it.

A question is a compliment!

Firstly, it is important to regard every question as a compliment and always leave enough time for them in your presentation.

Question time will be your chance to:

- ❑ **clarify your main points**
- ❑ **develop themes and add interest**
- ❑ **learn more about the subject and about the audience**
- ❑ **reinforce your main message and restate your 'call to arms'.**

Do not worry about question time – embrace it!
Questions are a gift … but only if you are prepared and able to deal with them!

Preparing for question time

Good preparation is key. It is imperative that you know your subject and audience and have thought through what is likely to be of interest or concern to them, so that you can also have planned your response.

As part of your preparation, and once you have completed your X-ray Sheet and constructed any support materials, look these over with a critical eye, from the audience's perspective.

Ask yourself:

- ❑ **Are there any gaps or threads left hanging?**
- ❑ **Are there any areas that do not link into the whole?**
- ❑ **Are there any areas that need to be handled carefully or sensitively?**
- ❑ **Are there any areas that I am worried about being challenged on?**
- ❑ **Do I have a 'nightmare question' that haunts me and really do not want to be asked?**

It is imperative that you think these through in advance. Do not be caught out or live in fear of what you *might* be asked. Address the challenge and be prepared for the worst question that you could be asked.

What are your nightmare questions?

_____

_____

_____

How will you respond to them?

_____

_____

_____

Self preservation

Before the event, decide on your attitude towards taking questions – do you have a policy? How do you want to manage them?

If you take questions during your presentation you will find the X-ray Sheet (see Chapter 1) invaluable in ensuring that you can deal with them and still manage your time so that you do not overrun.

Alternatively, you can take a question during your presentation and ask for permission to address it at the end. If you do this however, you must ensure that you leave sufficient time to deal with it fully.

Be clear about your brief – one way to ensure that you do not have to take questions that are outside your brief is to set clear parameters at the start of your presentation and as part of your introduction:

'This is me, these are my credentials. This is the subject of my presentation and this is my purpose in making it. I will be outlining ABC...' (and by implication therefore, will not be talking about XYZ).

It is quite useful at this stage to get the audience's agreement. This addresses any anticipation that they may have and forms a contract between you about how the presentation will run and what it will contain.

If you are presenting with a colleague, who will be talking about XYZ, then include that nugget of information in the opening piece. This will put the audience in the picture – make sure however, that your colleague is indeed covering this content, or your 'clear guidelines' might be later interpreted as passing the buck.

Anticipate questions – if you think that there are linked areas to which you might be taken, decide in advance whether you are prepared to go there and the depth to which you are able / qualified / empowered to do so.

Imagine that in a particular presentation and with a particular audience you might be asked by individuals who have functional responsibilities or particular interests to give some additional information about linked subjects which are relevant to them.

For example:

- ❑ Bob, the pragmatic Production Manager, is interested in implementation and might expect to see a case study.

- ❑ Silvia, the Financial Director, is interested in costs and would like some guide as to typical investment costs.

- ❑ Ollie, the Operations Manager, wants to understand specific products or services.

First, you must weigh up whether their question is one that you are willing and able to deal with. Will responding add value to your presentation? It may be that it does, or you feel that you have no choice but to address it anyway.

Next, decide whether this question is appropriate or of interest to everyone – this will help you to chose whether to give a 'top line', or a more detailed response. Will you address it now or later?

You are at the front of the room here and might be exposed if you are not prepared, or have not thought through, your tactics. There is no doubt that it is better to be over-prepared than under-prepared, and part of this could be to support your presentation with additional appendix material that you can draw on, if necessary.

Prepare your response and support materials – if you do decide to answer it, be aware that these linked areas or questions might each be a 'mini-presentation' in their own right. You can prepare and rehearse these and create supporting slides ready for use in your PowerPoint deck.

So for example, in dealing with Bob:

Bob: *'That's fine – but what experience does your company have of doing this?'*

Bob is asking about examples of specific implementation, but your expertise is in another niche area …

You: *'I was hoping that someone would ask that question. May I show you a list of our current partners?'*

(This is general 'top line' information – at the same time as you give it, bring up the appropriate PowerPoint slide – in this example, you press **100** and then press **Return** on your key board and up comes a slide showing client logos). Then continue:

        '… and if you like I can provide you with an outline case study …'

(That is your pre-prepared slide 101) … but, pause at this stage and check:

        '… is that relevant to everybody, or would you like me to send that information through / discuss it with you after this presentation?'

At this stage, the audience, the most senior person or your sponsor will make a call – but you have shown yourself to be knowledgeable, organised, in control and able to 'drill down' into specifics, if necessary.

How to get the first question

In some environments it will be easy to elicit questions, as audience members relish their chance to take the floor. On other occasions it can be more difficult to get the question process started. You are asking someone to give a mini-presentation – so if you want questions, make it easy for them!

❑ **Encourage questioners** – raise your own hand as a visual signal and move towards the audience, whilst asking for questions.

❑ **Do not expect instant questions** – allow the audience a few seconds to change gear from being passive listeners to active participants.

❑ **Plant the first question with your sponsor**, or perhaps even ask it of yourself:
- *'A question that I am sometimes asked is ...'*
- *'Someone asked me earlier ...'*
- *'What people normally want to know at this stage is ...'*

❑ **Hold back a question** asked during your presentation and begin with that:
- *'Now Bob, you were asking about ...'*

Ducking the question

A good-humoured response can often break tension – with the right audience an answer to a complicated question along the lines of:

❑ *'Would you like the long or the very long answer ...?'*

❑ *'I'm not sure that anyone has the answer to that ...'*

❑ *'Yes of course, that's the $64,000,000 question ...'*

... all of which prime the audience to be aware that you will not necessarily be able to answer that question here and now – it is too big; it is too complicated. The greatest thinkers in the world are still pondering it – and you are not going to provide an answer off the top of your head.

Blagging and winging it – under no circumstances should you attempt to bluff your way through a difficult question. At best, you will have managed to persuade people to believe something that you do not know to be true and at worst, you will have misled them and perhaps been found out in the process.

For example, we once attended a conference where the speaker was glibly talking about the team development stages of Tuckman's 1965 model of *Forming, Storming, Norming* and *Performing*. When asked what these headings meant, he thought for a moment and with an inspiration drawn from the ether, said with confidence:

> *'Oh, this has to do with the first Gulf War, where <u>Storming</u> <u>Norman</u> Schwarzkopf <u>formed</u> up the American forces, went to Iraq and <u>performed</u> really well ...'*

The third of the audience, who knew that this was complete gibberish, could not wait to tell the other two-thirds and the speaker's credibility evaporated, along with the impact of the rest of his presentation.

Keeping control of question time

Many people are afraid of question time – for the first time they are 'off script' and they fear losing control. There is no doubt that you must make sure that the show is still yours – even though question time offers others a cameo part in the limelight!

To manage the process, you might need to adjust your thinking and your role from that of presenter to chair, in order to facilitate discussion – but it is still up to you to direct proceedings and to keep control.

Remember to manage your body language and to keep watching the audience's. This will help you to judge the mood of the room and the relevance of particular questions, and will provide you with clues about how best to pitch your response.

Question types

There are many different sorts of question and questioners – each needs to be handled differently:

- ❑ **The question that is a statement** – some questioners are not looking for answers. They may be seeking approval, wanting to add value with an observation, or simply making a personal or political point. You should not expect every question to be a request for information. Thank the questioner for his or her contribution and move on.

- ❑ **The speech with no apparent question** – do not let the speech go on for too long – the audience will not thank you, indeed they may have heard this 'hobby-horse theme' before. Ask for clarity – what exactly is the question? If there is a question, answer it in the appropriate way – if there is no question, thank the questioner for the contribution and move on.

- ❑ **The multiple question** – you have no need to worry about these. Listen to the question and its subsidiaries – perhaps making a comment that you will answer one question at a time – and then answer the part of the question that you want to answer, which you are most able to answer, or which will have greatest value for the rest of the audience.

Then ask: *'Does that answer your question?'*

To which the answer will probably be:

'Yes, but not completely ...'

You can then take their next question (it is up to the questioner to remember what else they asked, not you!) and you can make a fresh decision about whether, or how, you want to answer it.

AARGH! THE DREADED 'MULTIPLE' QUESTION!

❑ **The irrelevant question** – gently point out to the questioner that their question is outside of the scope of your brief and of this presentation. If you can, direct them towards an answer – maybe a colleague, a web-site, or perhaps make a commitment to discuss it with them at the end of your presentation, or over coffee. If you make a commitment, you must deliver on it.

❑ **The question that you cannot answer** – if it is within your brief, there should be no such thing!

However, if you are uncomfortable because the question:

- relates to information you are not empowered to give out – say so!
- requires making a commitment on behalf of others that you cannot reasonably do – say so!
- involves something that you have not previously heard about, or been party to – say so!
- is in an area in which you do not have sufficient knowledge or information to give a definitive answer – say so!

Do not waffle or try to 'wing it'. Retain your credibility.

In order to move forward, perhaps check whether anyone else in the room has the answer, or is more qualified than you to respond – in other words throw it open to the floor.

If not, simply say:

'I'll find out and I will get back to you.'

Offer your contact details, take theirs and commit to a time by when you will get back to them.

Check whether the rest of the audience need the answer as well and if they do, organise the logistics accordingly.

❑ **The question that is really a 'heckle'** – do not let negative body language or negative comments from the audience throw you. Keep your cool, be calm, be reasonable, be polite – all of these things will demonstrate your confidence and will be likely to bring the audience on to your side, if they are not there already.

If the heckler continues, do not try to compete and certainly do not get involved in an argument. Perhaps agree to differ, or offer to discuss the matter privately, or in a different forum. Thank them for their observation and in the same breath move on to ask for any other questions from the rest of the audience.

Good question-handling practice

Do not get bogged down on one question, or let one person from the audience monopolise question time – aim to achieve a fair distribution of questions and questioners.

❑ **Although you will take a question from one person** – make your answer to the whole room.

❑ **If several hands go up, impose the order in which you will take questions** – the audience will remember the 'order of appearance'. You will have established your authority and removed the distraction of waving hands.

❑ **If you are not clear about a question, check your understanding** – and re-state or summarise it if you think it has not been heard by everyone.

❑ **Correct inaccuracies of fact if necessary** – do not automatically accept the wording of a question, or the bias of a questioner's point of view.

Keeping to time

There is seldom much time for questions and excessive detail in your reply will lead to frustration, so keep your answers short and to the point – unless you want to use them as a spring board to talk about something else, which is key to your agenda.

If there are so many questions or interruptions that it looks as though you may overrun, note the fact and check with your audience and sponsor whether you should bring questions to an end. Many of the audience will be grateful!

Finishing on a positive note

Remember to thank people for their questions, and then to reclaim the floor and re-emphasise your key points.

Whatever happens during question time, it is vital that the audience leaves with your key 5% of points resounding in their ears.

❑ **You must be remembered for the right reasons.**

❑ **Have your summary visual and your final statement (your 'call to arms') ready for the end.**

❑ It is imperative that yours is the last message that the audience sees and hears.

End on a positive, planned note and the audience will be more inclined to remember it as having been a positive and well planned presentation.

Questions in other environments

There will be many other occasions when you will be expected to draw upon your question handling skills – for example if you are invited on to an 'expert panel' at a conference, or trade show stand.

There are several key differences between handling questions as part of delivering a presentation and being questioned 'cold'.

In a presentation:

❑ you set the agenda.

❑ you have the floor pretty well unchallenged.

❑ you have the right to direct affairs and are in control.

In a 'question taking environment':

❑ you do not set the agenda.

❑ every statement you make can be challenged.

❑ you cannot direct affairs and are not in control, unless you handle the questioning process in the right way.

If you are in a public forum or in an environment where you do not know who is asking the questions or what their agenda might be, your responses need to be truthful, accurate and well thought through.

This is not an environment in which to 'wing it', 'knock' the opposition, or offer any 'off the cuff' remark that might be used as a sound bite.

What do visitors to a trade show or open forum want when they ask questions?

❑ a good entertaining interaction.

❑ new and up-to-date information.

❑ the chance to tell you their 'war stories'.

❑ a chance to show off in front of their peers / friends.

What do you want? Probably:

❑ to put yourself and your message in the public domain, in a positive light and with a higher profile.

❑ an opportunity to correct misconceptions / mistakes.

❑ to be first choice whenever the questioner wants someone to talk with authority about your area of expertise in the future.

If you are putting yourself in the position of someone of whom questions can be asked, you must:

❑ **know your subject** – think through the questions that you are likely to be asked and be aware that the session may open up into more general and controversial areas – so, have your responses prepared.

❑ **be helpful** – provide information and answer the questions asked, in a conversational way.

❑ **be concise and jargon free.**

❑ **provide appropriate well thought out examples.**

❑ **make sure that you are 'up to date'** – and at least as well-informed about current issues and developments as the people in the room are.

❑ **be energetic, enthusiastic and engaging** – and …

… roll with the hits and keep both your sense of perspective and sense of humour!

We have already said that a well-prepared presentation is 90% given. In the same way, preparation is essential when you make yourself available as a representative speaker for your company or for your ideas.

The Four Corner-stones

ONE
THE PURPOSE
WHY?

TWO
THE AUDIENCE
WHO?

THREE
THE CONTENT
WHAT?

FOUR
THE BEST MEDIUM
HOW?

If you are doing a trade show or sitting on an expert panel, you need to be clear on several points.

❑ **Why are you making yourself available?** – What is your reason for being there?

❑ **Who will the audience be?** – Trade professional, general public, press?

❑ **What are you going to say?** – Do you have a point of view and agenda?

❑ **How are you going to say it?** – Will you adopt a 'role'?

Stand & Deliver

'Link' expressions

Being on a panel is a little like being interviewed and it is sometimes worthwhile trying to move the questions towards the answers that **you** want to give. This is achieved through using link expressions.

The idea is to pick up on a key word or phrase in the question which you can use to divert the question in the direction that **you** want it to go. You can also use link expressions to get back on track, particularly if the questioner is trying to lead you somewhere that you do not want to go.

'Link' expressions examples:

- ❏ *Ah yes, but that's only half the story ...'*
- ❏ *'What everyone is forgetting ...?'*
- ❏ *'What a lot of people don't know ...'*
- ❏ *'If we look at the most recent developments ...'*
- ❏ *'... leading on from this, is the more relevant point of ...'*
- ❏ *'... and I believe this has been covered well, but what has received little attention is ...'*
- ❏ *'... but the real debate should be about ...'*
- ❏ *'... that's a really interesting point and of course it is closely linked to ...'*
- ❏ *'... our research and practical experience suggests ...'*

Messages

It is also smart to think through in advance what your proactive message will be. What are the key points that you want to get across in this forum, even if no-one asks you!? If you do not know, you are very unlikely to find a way to get them in, or use the event to full advantage!

Why not:

- ❏ identify a maximum of two or three points that you want to get across.
- ❏ put your messages in order of importance. Never leave the most vital point to the end – you might never get there!
- ❏ identify your audience. What would interest them? Find an appropriate story, or a case study to use as a vehicle.

Staying focused on your key messages and finding link phrases that work for you, are great allies whenever you are in the position of taking questions and are well worth practising.

Section 4

Chapter 10

Managing the Environment and Room Set-up

- Seizing control
- Choosing the room
- Room sizes
- Room layout
- The worst rooms
- 'Fixed' boardrooms

- Organising your session
- Personalise the environment
- Presenting 1:1
- Personal set-up checklist
- Personal equipment list

Seizing control

Something that is very often overlooked by presenters – who otherwise might make great presentations – is the environment into which the audience will be coming, the style in which the room is set up and the arrangements that have been made to ensure the comfort and safety of the audience.

These are all areas where knowing what you want, combined with a little preparation, can make a huge difference to the outcomes achieved.

The reality is that as the presenter, people will hold you responsible for any aspect of the venue that is not 'up to the mark' and a badly thought-out venue will impact on your ability to deliver a successful presentation.

It is very unlikely that anyone else will notice your efforts in getting things right, although they will notice if things are *not* right – so your attention to detail *will* definitely pay off!

If you are hosting your presentation in a public place then you have some added responsibility and should check out the location of toilets, the provisions that have been made for smokers, and fire escape routes – all information that you should pass on to your audience.

Choosing the room

Try to get a room where there is natural light – but be aware of windows and reflected light on your screen – make sure that there are blinds, should sunlight or outside activity necessitate their use.

Make sure that you can control the heating and ventilation. In hotels and conference centres there is often a centralised heating control and your needs, presenting to a group of 12 for example, will be different to another group holding a dinner dance at the same time!

If you are presenting 'in-house', make sure that the room is booked for as long as you need it, has equipment that works and is large enough for your requirements.

Administrators are often unaware of how much space will be required and hotels and conference centres often promote whichever room suits them! However, do speak to the hotel for guidance, because the number of people a room will take is very dependent on the room layout.

Room sizes

As a guide, we would recommend for a:

Group of 6	-	4m x 7m	Group of 50	-	13m x 10m
Group of 12	-	7m x 7m	Group of 100	-	13m x 20m
Group of 25	-	10m x 7m			

Room layout

Wherever possible, check out the presentation space in advance and always endeavour to get access to it early enough to set up at leisure on the day of the presentation.

If you are presenting in someone else's offices or location, then you are in their hands – but knowing your requirements and expressing them clearly will make it more likely that you and the audience will be better served.

If your presentation is taking place over a sustained period, make sure that drinks, sweets and possibly fresh fruit are available in the room and that refreshments are also available, outside of the room, during breaks.

Breakout rooms, or the option of going outside for activities, can also offer a welcome change of scene.

If you have the opportunity to choose and set up the room to suit yourself, then always do so. This will make the room 'your room' and you will be more comfortable in the knowledge that you have set it up in a way that is best suited to you and to your message.

Consider in advance the room layout that will add most value to your presentation. What atmosphere do you want to create? Are you having:

- ❑ a lecture?
- ❑ a meeting with the board?
- ❑ a free-flowing discussion?

Consider how your set-up will be affected by the number of people attending and by the style of your presentation.

What set-up would be most useful in running the discussions, or activities that you have planned to use?

The choices that you make about the way that you arrange the room will give out signals to your listeners, even as they arrive.

Room set-up is often dictated by the placing of the projection screen. There are two main options: Off-set screen and Head-on screen.

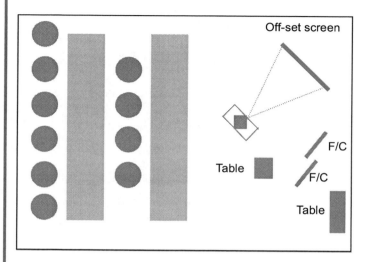

Figure 1

If the screen is off-set (Figure 1), the audience will be able to look at you or the screen, but not both. This set-up works well if you use a remote control for the PowerPoint, because you have room to move around in the remaining two-thirds of space at the front of the room.

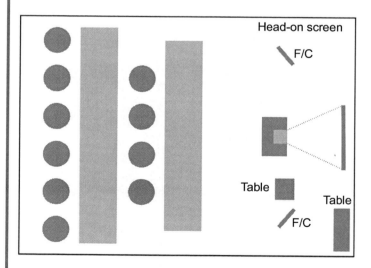

Figure 2

If the screen is head-on, however, the audience can see you and the visual at the same time, but your space for movement is limited and many presenters tend to get trapped in the bottom right quadrant, shown in Figure 2.

If you are using flipcharts as well, they need to be placed carefully, so that they are out of the way when not needed, but in everyone's line of sight when they are.

Think about how you want to move around at the front of the room. Use the flipchart that is hardest to access for static data (for example, an agenda) and the one that you can access more easily, and which the audience can see more clearly, for live diagrams and build-up work.

Alternative room set-ups – seating arrangements affect the way an audience responds to you and to each other. Many hotel and conference venues will set a room up in a way that suits them, often dictated by the number and shape of tables that they have available!

Be very clear about your needs and strive to get the best that you can for your audience.

Smaller groups – for smaller groups (8 – 16) and an open atmosphere use the round table or open circle layouts.

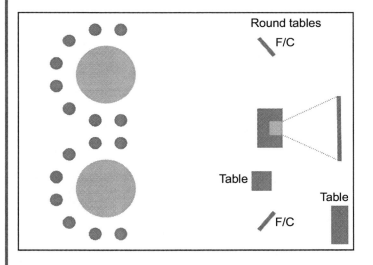

Figure 3

Round tables (Figure 3) are great if you want the audience to interact with each other and with you, or if you want to move into small group work or discussion.

Open-circle layout (Figure 4) – with or without tables – provides the audience with the opportunity to see you and each other, but it is less good for moving into small group work.

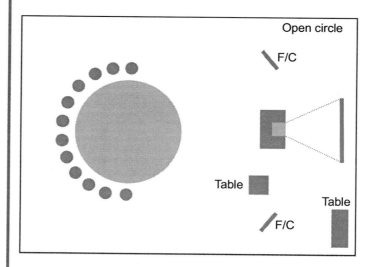

Figure 4

Medium-sized groups – for medium sized groups (16 – 30) use the horseshoe, adjusted horse shoe or block style.

The horseshoe (Figure 5) provides great visibility for the audience to see the front of the room. It is useful if you want to facilitate general 'whole group' discussion, but less good for moving into small group work.

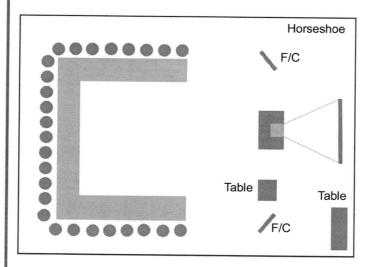

Figure 5

We favour the adjusted horseshoe variant (Figure 6) because having fewer delegates in the bottom quadrant makes it possible for the presenter to move into the audience more easily.

We have also seen one presenter who uses an office chair with wheels to allow him to move around at pace inside the horseshoe! Although this was unusual, it was thoroughly enjoyed by the participants, who loved the idea of him being able to move around and give individuals or small groups very close attention, whenever he was asking for their ideas and opinions.

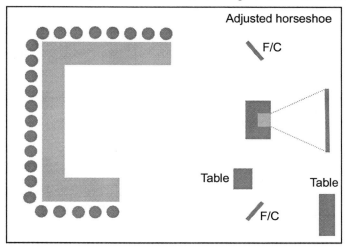

Figure 6

The block style (Figure 7) is less common and also less good for allowing audience members a clean line of sight. For this reason, we would always recommend using round tables as shown in Figure 3.

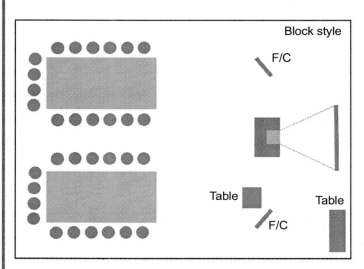

Figure 7

Larger groups – when tables are needed for larger groups (25 or over), use conference, cabaret or herringbone layout. These layouts can be easily adapted to different room sizes and, if necessary, the tables can be removed and the same patterns followed.

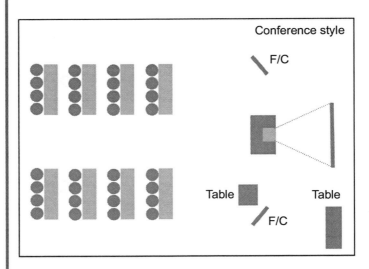

Figure 8

Many audience members find the Conference style (Figure 8) and Herringbone style (Figure 9) reminiscent of school – they seem regimented and restricted. For this reason alone, we would not recommend either. However, because it is hard for people to talk with anyone but their immediate neighbours, it is useful if you want to keep control and have the focus of their attention to be the front of the room!

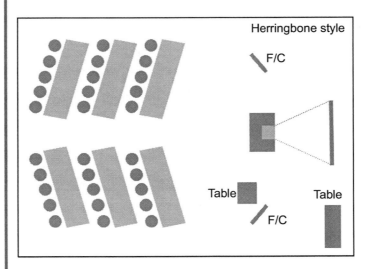

Figure 9

Cabaret style (Figure 10) is a more open and 'friendly' set-up. It is not as restricting as Conference or Herringbone and easily lends itself to moving into small group work.

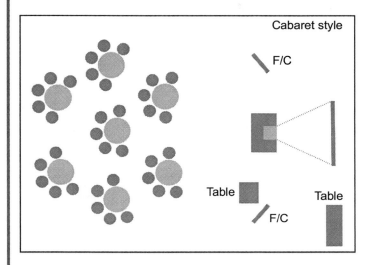

Figure 10

For larger groups or public speaking – in a conference hall or lecture theatre – the seats and the staging are likely to be fixed, or at least have been predetermined in theatre style. Work with the conference centre staff and they will help you to get the best from the venue, offering assistance with any technology, microphones and the lectern. Use the microphone if one is provided (see Chapter 8).

With larger groups, if you have dispensed with tables, you may also choose to use Theatre style, Semi-circle or Circle.

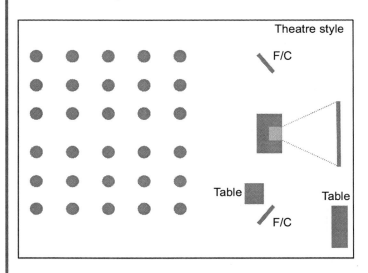

Figure 11

Theatre style (Figure 11) is quick to set-up and works well if a lot of people need to fit in a room and be addressed by an individual or a panel, without the need for interaction amongst themselves.

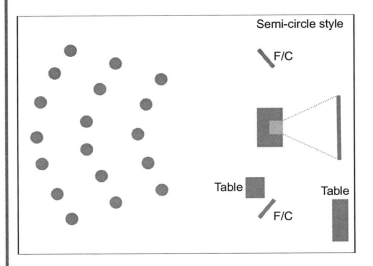

Figure 12

Figure 13 has dispensed not only with tables, but also with the screen and projector, providing an air of spontaneity and informality. As a result, these are both good formats to use if you want to encourage discussion and contributions from the audience.

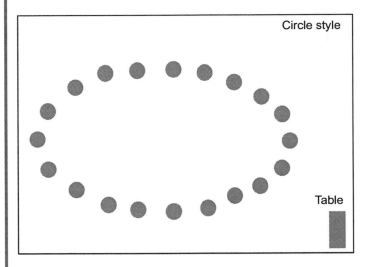

Figure 13

Be aware that in some cultures, however, a circle of chairs smacks a little of 'group therapy' sessions and will need to be positioned carefully!

When working with large groups, it could also be worthwhile to consider using staging at the front of the room to elevate you, your screen and your flipcharts – making them all more visible to people at the back of the room.

The worst rooms

The worst rooms have low ceilings, no natural light, poor ventilation and someone else's hand on the temperature control! Pillars will obscure the viewing lines and having too little room to be comfortable will make the room feel claustrophobic.

Try not to make presentations in the subterranean environment; it does not add much value. Never be afraid to ask for a different room!

'Fixed' boardrooms

Boardrooms with fixed tables (Figure 14) can also be difficult, as they tend to be long and thin and it is easier for people to have conversations across the table, than it is for them to see you, your flipcharts or the screen, if you present from one end.

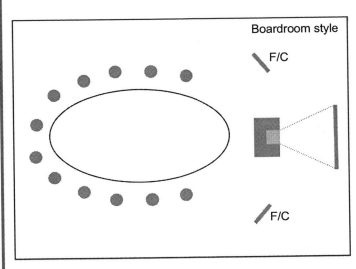

Figure 14

Change the environment – consider rearranging things so that you present from one side, as in Figure 15.

If nothing else, this will let people know that your presentation is something different. It will open things out and draw everyone's attention towards you, whilst giving them much better lines of sight.

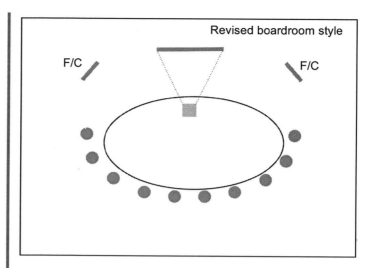

Figure 15

Always consider the most advantageous layout for you and your audience and be prepared to adjust the room accordingly.

Personalise the environment

If you have no control over the room layout, then at least try to personalise it in some way. Perhaps have music, or a rolling PowerPoint presentation playing as people arrive.

You could have some pre-prepared flipcharts, or a welcome visual, or a quote showing, to let people know that they are in the right place and can expect something different and interesting.

❑ **Check signage** – this will ensure that your audience can find you and, by including a start time and an earlier meeting time, you will help them to be on time.

Organising your session

❑ **Welcome the audience members as they arrive** – this allows you to:

- make personal contact
- find out their names
- find out where they are from
- find out about any specific areas of knowledge or expertise that they may have
- link your presentation to them – make them an ally, a friendly face in the room from the outset.

This will also help you to:

❑ **Fill from the front and the centre** – otherwise you will find that most audiences – especially in large auditoriums – fill from the back and spread out, making them harder to work as a group.

❑ **Have a welcome pack** – what do you need the audience to know? Can you use this to re-confirm the parameters of your presentation, to give extra detail, a sample, or your contact details? People love a take-away.

❑ **Provide name badges and name cards** – this will help you to:

- remember who people are and to use their names and titles.
- add branding to an event (why advertise the venue?).
- show your attention to detail.

❑ **Make sure the audience will be comfortable**

- Check out the furniture – make sure that the tables and chairs are fit for purpose.
- Ensure that there are writing materials and water available.
- Allow time for comfort or 'bio' breaks.

❑ **Arrange for refreshments to be available during the breaks** – if possible, this should be outside of the main room, which allows for a change of scenery for the audience and gives you space to gather your thoughts and prepare the next session in private.

Beware, do not let the audience wander too far – give clear guidelines as to your restart times and establish good practice by starting on time, every time.

❑ **Make sure that the room is lockable** – it may not be your job to be responsible for security, but if you are intending to take breaks that will leave the room empty and something goes missing, it will undoubtedly affect the next part of your presentation.

Presenting 1:1

When presenting 1:1 and using your PC, try to sit side by side, or across the corner of a desk, jointly looking at the screen. Sitting face to face across the desk can feel adversarial.

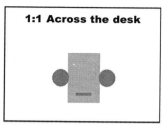

1:1 Across the desk

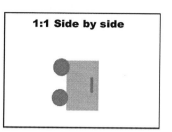

1:1 Side by side

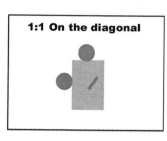

1:1 On the diagonal

If you are a guest and presenting on someone else's 'patch', they may have an opinion as to how they want things to be set up, but nudge them towards the most beneficial format.

Make sure that your PC screen and keyboard are clean and that your screen saver is appropriate to the business environment.

Personal set-up checklist

Prepare an action list for your venue and set-up preferences.

_____

_____

_____

_____

Personal equipment list

Prepare an equipment list to ensure that you always have everything that you need in your 'presenter kit'.

_____

_____

_____

_____

Add to these lists over time and use them as checklists before any presentation.

Section 4

Chapter 11

Advanced Tactics

- Non-standard issues

- Conference speaking

- Presenting to a board

- Presenting in-house

- Presenting bad news

- Coping with hostility

- Presenting with others

- Presenting an existing deck

- 'Just send me your PowerPoint slides...'

- Gisting

- Presenting 1:1

- Checklists

- Keeping control

Non-standard issues

On most occasions you will be presenting alone and will be able to dictate the style and set-up of your presentation. On other occasions you will be expected to fall in line with others – perhaps as a speaker at a conference, to a board where there is a pre-set format, or delivering as part of a team. There may also be occasions when you are required to deliver bad news, deal with hostility or deliver somebody else's presentation – possibly using an already existing PowerPoint deck or other visuals.

This final chapter is aimed at addressing all of these 'non-standard issues', as well as introducing the idea of 'Gisting', and it offers guidance on how to respond when people request a copy of your PowerPoint – which will happen – as many people believe that the PowerPoint **is** your presentation and that it can succinctly summarise everything that you wanted it to say.

So, in turn:

Conference speaking

This is one of the rare occasions where a speech delivered verbatim is acceptable – indeed if the content is sensitive, or needs to be translated – it may even be a requirement – which, if nothing else, will guarantee that you will finish on time!

Big conference venues cope well with technology and this is a good opportunity to use the internet, DVD or other pre-prepared interventions as part of your presentation. Be guided by the organisers. Use a microphone and consider using AutoCue, if they are provided (see Chapter 8). If you are trying new things, rehearse fully.

Work closely with the technicians and they will help you. Let them know if you intend to do anything out of the ordinary, or which needs support from their lighting, or sound systems.

Conference audiences often enjoy anything that is different or distinctive, (so long as it is still relevant) – so, do not be afraid to break with convention. The response from a large group can be slightly slower compared to that of a small group – it is nonetheless equally, if not *more,* gratifying. Use big gestures and build in pauses for response – do not be tempted to talk over applause or laughter. Enjoy it!

If you want to move around the podium and away from the lectern you will need a lapel mike and, if you want to be interactive with the audience, there will need to be a roving mike available so that their voices can also be amplified.

You will probably be introduced by the organisers or chairperson – make sure that they have an up-to-date and relevant CV, so that they can build your credibility.

'It is always much more effective if someone else will blow your trumpet for you.'
Anon

Linking in to other speakers

If you are following on from previous speakers, try to 'sit in' on their input, so that you do not embarrass yourself by unwittingly repeating or contradicting their points. Instead, use the time to 'tune in' to the atmosphere, so that you are able to demonstrate empathy by linking back and making connections with things that have previously been said or debated.

Presenting to a board

If you have been asked to present to a board, or to a senior team, it will be because they believe that you have something worthwhile to say to them – which is a great starting point and should give you personal confidence!

☐ **Do not be overawed** by either the opportunity or the environment – but do make sure that you show deference to the culture and respect for the members of the audience, individually.

☐ **Whatever the mood in the room** when you enter, remember that you are an outsider, in a political environment.

All of the tools and techniques outlined in *Stand & Deliver* so far will help you to prepare yourself for this presentation, but beware! On these kind of occasions, you are unlikely to be able to re-arrange the presenting environment to suit yourself; senior people are quite likely to change the duration of your presentation and where it appears in their agenda at very short notice – so you must be flexible – and, although you can outline your question-taking policy, they are very likely to do whatever suits them!

Stay close to your sponsor! They will help you to stay on track.

Before the event:

☐ **Confirm the purpose** – what are the expected outcomes from your presentation?

☐ **Find out about the audience** – what will they need and expect from you? Who will make the decisions? Based on what criteria?

☐ **Run through your content with your sponsor** – provide a top-level or 'Gisted' overview (see page 159) to find out if it is it on the right lines. Does it seem that you are intending to deliver your message in a way that this group will find palatable?

☐ **Check the provision of equipment** – find out if you will be able to use PowerPoint and whether the screen and data projector will already be set up. Will you be able to use your own PC, or will you have to submit your presentation in advance? Confirm the dress code. Your sponsor will be in a position to give you a great steer.

If you are setting up your own equipment – go for speed and efficiency. Save the music and the video clips for another day. This is not the best time to try anything new or risky – keep things simple!

At the event

☐ If you are met by your sponsor in reception or on the way to the meeting room, use the time to find out any up-to-the-minute information that may help you. Do not be afraid to make further adjustments to your content or style that receiving this information may prompt.

Entering the room

☐ On entering the room let your sponsor take the lead, and only if they do not, then take the initiative. This includes:

- thanking your sponsor
- greeting the group
- thanking the board for giving you the opportunity to speak with them
- introducing yourself and setting up your equipment with the minimum of fuss
- when you are set, use the Ready Position (see page 40) to get centred, take a breath, and begin with your introduction.

Beginning your presentation

☐ Include:
- a grab
- the purpose for the presentation
- your credentials
- the intended outcomes
- ask for agreement of the time and other parameters (including your question-taking preferences).

Make sure that your presentation has something of interest for everyone. As always, take questions from one person, but address your answer to the whole group.

After questions, summarise and give your closing grab, or make a request for agreement as to the next steps. Thank the group, thank your sponsor and stand to one side.

It will be made clear to you whether you should now stay, or beat a retreat!

Presenting in-house

In-house presentations can be less formal affairs, but they should be no less professional in their preparation or delivery. Think of this as another opportunity to market yourself and your ideas and do everything you need to set yourself for success.

Make sure that the room and equipment is booked and that you are not gazumped by others who may also want to use the same facilities.

Presenting bad news

❑ **Presenting bad news brings it own challenges** – if there have been rumours beforehand, it is important to ensure that you get your information out in a clear, concise and unambiguous way. Err on the side of formality.

❑ **Decide on your question-taking policy** – tell the audience how you would like to deliver your message up front. It is much better to get your points out without interruptions, if possible. Allow ample time for questions and make sure that you have the correct people and information on hand to give the appropriate answers.

❑ **Set clear parameters of what you can and cannot say** – have a look at the section on link expressions and messages in Chapter 9 – and think through your responses in advance. Do not be pushed into saying more than you intended.

❑ **If you are delivering bad news and you think that the reaction may be verbally or physically challenging** – make sure that you have other people to support you in the room – perhaps organise yourself as part of a 'panel', which will give you a bigger and more unified stage presence.

Coping with hostility

On this or other occasions, a presentation may give rise to strong feelings or opposing viewpoints amongst the audience.

If you and your subject matter are the focus of the discontent, be very clear about why you are there and what you have been tasked to deliver. Be assertive in outlining the parameters of your remit and do not allow yourself to be pulled off course, or into an argument. Address the whole audience with your reply and avoid prolonged eye contact with any individual protagonist, as this can be interpreted as aggression.

You might suggest that if an individual's discomfort precludes them from listening to your points, they might like to withdraw – as clearly one of you is in the wrong room!

If the debate is within the audience, you can act as facilitator (although many will probably see your role as that of mediator).

Remember, however, that this is your presentation and bring it back on track as soon as possible.

It is up to you to re-focus all participants, so thank the protagonists, acknowledge their strong views and the importance of the matter and suggest that the debate should be saved for another time or place, or will be addressed later in the presentation, or as part of question time.

Dealing with an aggressive, dominating person – if an audience member is aggressive and attempts to dominate or override your presentation:

- ❑ **keep the conversation between you formal.**
- ❑ **let them make their points.**
- ❑ **seek clarity and factual information.**
- ❑ **respond with concise, clear, factual comments.**
- ❑ **focus on creating positive results and outcomes.**
- ❑ **give some options for a short term resolution that will enable you to proceed with your presentation.**

Stay focused on the bigger picture and know when to drop an issue, or to seek help from others.

Being assertive – if you are sitting down, stand up to reassert your authority. Remind the audience of the presentation's purpose and demonstrate that you are in control.

Handling the situation well will add to your overall credibility and your own confidence. Invariably you will find that the rest of the audience will swing to your side and respect your control and authority.

Presenting with others

On some occasions, it will be necessary to present with others, or as part of a team. This requirement may be imposed upon you or it may be your preference – allowing you to draw upon different expertise. Either way, it is important to establish some conventions, ground rules and roles.

As a guide, the fewer presenters the better – two is better than six! No matter the number, try to vary personalities and styles. Play to your individual strengths and draw together a team where the overall impact of combined skills and approaches are complementary.

The extent to which you gel as a team, before, during and after the presentation will be apparent to your audience and will have an impact on how they respond to you and your message. Your ability to support each other and 'pass the baton' between you will effect how 'tight', well-ordered and rounded the presentation feels.

Try to behave as if you like, trust and value each other's contributions!

Decide and agree tactics – if you are presenting with one or more other people, you must be absolutely clear at the outset about the purpose and objectives – so that the message is focused and consistent throughout.

- ❑ **Decide how you will create the presentation** – will one person create the whole, or will each individual develop their own section?

- ❑ **Appoint a lead presenter** – they will need to lead the planning process, to identify who is going to say what and gain everyone's agreement that they are empowered to make 'executive decisions' to keep things moving during the presentation.

  They will need to chair the presentation and choreograph the event, managing the sequence, the timings and taking a lead if plans need to change.

  It may also fall to them to introduce everyone at the beginning of the presentation and 'set the scene', so that the audience is clear about each person's role and area of expertise.

Having clear parameters will also make things much easier at question time.

☐ **Consider how you will handle visual aids** – you may want to have one person to operate the PowerPoint, or take it in turns to operate it for each other.

If one person is facilitating a flipchart session, another colleague could be used as a scribe, to capture ideas and information.

☐ **Decide amongst yourselves when and how you will take questions** – tell the audience your preference at the start, but remember you may need to be flexible.

Anticipate what questions might be asked and decide who is best suited to answer which.

☐ **Rehearse** – practise together before the event – allow time for a 'stumble through', a 'run through' and a dress rehearsal, so that the themes, handovers and transitions are smooth and the 'red thread' is clear.

Definitely rehearse your opening and how you will hand over to each other. Avoid swapping over too often, as this can make it difficult for the audience to follow.

Think through and practise a strong summary and close.

Each presenter should be able to deliver the whole presentation, so that you do not have a problem if one person is unavailable, for any reason.

Stage management

Think through your choreography and stage management. For example, will everyone stand or sit? Be clear about your preferences and your response to different circumstances.

☐ **Consider how you will be dressed** – it might look inappropriate if one of you is dressed formally and another casually.

☐ **Stagecraft** – while a colleague is speaking, make sure that you are paying attention to them. It is easy to be thinking about what you are about to say and not listening to what is happening around you. The audience will pick up on this and your body language may be interpreted as a lack of interest or respect.

The colleague who is speaking should be the most important and interesting person in the room(!) – and your body language should be supportive and encouraging of them. Laugh at their jokes, look concerned in the serious bits and nod thoughtfully when they make a good point.

☐ **Stay on message** – if you disagree with something that a colleague says, do not fall out in public. If everyone stays 'on message', there should be no surprises.

Presenting an existing deck

On occasions, you may be asked to present on someone else's behalf. Our experience is that either they have done no work at all on preparing the presentation, or the request is preceeded by the words:

'Could you just ...'

In which case you need to begin your preparation with the Four Cornerstones and by creating an X-ray Sheet.

Alternatively, they will supply a pre-prepared deck, which they will give to you with the implication that:

'All you have to do is deliver it ...'

If your presence adds no value to the proposed PowerPoint presentation – why don't they just email it to the audience members?

As this option is not usually chosen, clearly there is an assumption that your presence will add value – your task is to make sure that it does!!

The advantages of using pre-prepared PowerPoint decks

Some organisations have a huge bank of pre-prepared decks. In the ideal world this makes sense, because these decks are:

- ❑ corporate
- ❑ branded
- ❑ legally correct
- ❑ well thought through and structured
- ❑ up-to-date

They will contain good graphics and visuals... and they save you re-inventing the wheel.

The disadvantages of using a pre-existing deck

In many cases, especially if the deck has been designed to introduce a product or service, or outline a particular solution, they are likely to be:

- ❑ generic
- ❑ all-encompassing
- ❑ over-full with information
- ❑ too wordy
- ❑ full of complex graphics
- ❑ over-full with a high number of slides

A further disadvantage is that they will not always be structured in a way that is logical to everyone and, because no-one 'owns' them, will not necessarily be up-to-date.

This often leads to presenters of these slides beginning their presentation with:

'I have been asked to make this presentation …' (Real message: 'Don't shoot me, I'm only the messenger – in fact I'm just a late stand in, brought in off the streets…')

Or: *'This isn't my deck …'* (Real message: 'I don't own or take any responsibility for this content – in fact I may not even understand it and the next slide will be as much of a surprise to me as it is to you…')

Which must be the two opening phrases any audience member least want to hear!

Going back to fundamentals

If you are asked to make a presentation on someone else's behalf, it is imperative to re-visit the Four Corner-stones and check that you have the answers to the fundamental questions:

Why am I making this presentation?

Who am I making this presentation to?

What is the relevant content?

How am I going to say it?

Once you have answered these questions, it is worthwhile looking through the pre-prepared PowerPoint and asking:

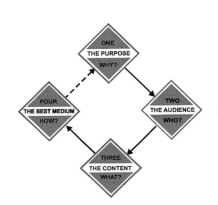

'Which part of this will help me to achieve the above?'

Now re-develop the PowerPoint!

You will need to cut, re-order, edit and add your own slides to create a deck that supports *your* message and which you are proud to own – a process which we call 'Gisting' (see below).

You may of course also choose to include other useful supporting tactics (metaphor, analogy, case studies – see Chapter 7), which the pre-prepared deck could never cater for. This will position you to deliver a presentation that is successful and memorable and from which you and your message will gain credibility – not least because your work will have ensured that the presentation has been delivered with professional impact.

This also leads us on to the issue of receiving a request for a copy of your deck.

'Just send me your PowerPoint slides …'

How often have you been asked for a copy of your PowerPoint presentation?

A fear of this request often drives people to have a lot of bullet points, or to include too many 'wordy' slides in their presentation – so that it can be understood without its most essential ingredient – *You!*

Is that the purpose of your PowerPoint?

Distinguish between the hard (written) data that you want to communicate and the verbal presentation that you are going to deliver.

Many people assume that having a copy of a PowerPoint deck will provide an eloquent summary of what the presentation had to say, but unless the presentation was written with this express outcome in mind, it is very unlikely that the PowerPoint alone can convey the whole story.

Every request for a copy of your deck will require a different response and in fact how you react will always be subjective.

As a starting point, consider who is asking for your deck and what is behind their request.

Thinking this through may well lead you into responding differently on each occasion.

❏ **Your manager or a colleague requests your deck in order to check or add content to your presentation.**

In general, your manager or colleague will need to see your X-ray Sheet and PowerPoint together, if they are to get the 'full picture' of what you intend to present. This will need to happen before the event and be part of the creative process.

❏ **An audience member asks for a copy of your deck, because they do not want to make notes during the presentation or cannot attend.**

If a person wants to avoid making notes and is simply requesting an historical record of what you intend to say, then having pre-prepared handouts (either a summary or something which offers additional information), may be all that you need to have available to match their request. This would certainly work if this was a 'just for your information' type presentation.

Alternatively, providing your PowerPoint and speaker notes may satisfy their need, but be aware that these can only represent what you intended to say and show, and may not record the presentation that you actually delivered. Neither does it record the questions that the audience were prompted to ask, or the dialogue that took place.

By simply passing on the PowerPoint deck you could well be missing an opportunity!

We strongly recommend that if your presentation was in any way 'live and interactive' – and definitely for the person who is unable to attend your presentation, but wants to understand what they missed – you should forward a Word document, incorporating selected PowerPoint visuals, plus a record of any discussion, agreed action points and a summary of the next steps.

This turns their request of 'Can I have a copy of your deck?' into a much more proactive and forward-looking communications process. Rather than just providing a record of your visuals, you have instead given them a summary of the 'story so far', bringing them completely up to date.

Editing into Word also protects your original presentation from being circulated or used without your permission.

Gisting

Gisting is a process for taking a chunk of words or data and bringing them down to the essence of their meaning – with the intention of making the whole easier to communicate.

The root of gisting

We first developed gisting when working with an international Bank, who were trying to cascade communications to local subsidiaries by sending a bulky 'comms pack' to regionally based spokespeople, who were expected to deliver the information to managers, in a lively and interesting way.

Although we were initially asked to help these people with their presentation skills, we quickly realised that a major stumbling block for them was **What** they were expected to communicate, as much as **How** they would present it.

The content was dry, unexciting and often overly complex – and simply reading it from the page made for a dry, dull and often overly complex communications session!

The benefits of gisting

We encouraged these spokespeople to distil the information, to re-order the content and humanise it – at a stroke, making it easier to deliver and more relevant and accessible to the local constituency. The communication still retained the key messages – producing a process which came to be known as 'gisting'.

By combining the editor's pencil with the Four Corner-stones and using the X-ray Sheet as a script, generic content can be made more interesting, the deliverer's role more worthwhile and the communication itself will be more successfully delivered.

Presenting 1:1

'Just give me the summary ... the gist of your presentation.'

Often managers, sponsors or colleagues will ask for a 'heads up' on a presentation that is about to be delivered. Having used the colour coded X-ray Sheet in the preparation process pays great dividends here, because it is a tool that really lends itself to delivering a gisted presentation, of any length.

Headings are in black and 'must have' information is in red and running through these together provides the headline or executive summary (the gist) of a 1 hour presentation in 2 or 3 minutes – with the guarantee that all of the salient points are included!

Drilling for detail – if the manager or sponsor chooses to drill down in any area, then explaining the blue input ('I have a story to explain that ...', 'I intend to use a PowerPoint slide to capture the bullet point summary of advantages ...', 'I was going to draw the XYZ model on the flipchart to emphasise that ...') and having the green 'nice to have content' to add detail will really make you appear to be in control of your content.

Stand & Deliver

Checklists

Personal Checklist

In the weeks and days before a presentation:

PLAN
↓
PREPARE
↓
PRACTISE
↓
PERFORM

☐ **Remember the 4 Ps** – plan and prepare thoroughly and in good time.

☐ Use the Four Corner-stones – to create firm foundations for your presentation.

☐ **Make sure your presentation matches the brief** – it should be relevant, straightforward and to the point. Simplify complex ideas and add highlights and 'magic'.

☐ **Prepare support materials** – handouts, PowerPoint and any other visual supports. Unless you are running Presenter View in PowerPoint (see page 113) print off your own PowerPoint slides (9 to a page and number them) for easy reference during the presentation.

☐ **Allow enough time for preparation and practice** – it is impossible to say how long preparation will take – it will be influenced by the subject matter, your level of expertise in the area and how proficient you want the output to be. But, better to be over prepared and rehearsed than to be found wanting!

☐ **Identify potential interruptions and problems** – ask yourself 'What if?' and prepare your responses.

☐ **Decide what you are going to wear in advance** – so that you can ensure that it is available and clean.

☐ **Practise, practise, practise your presentation** – do this out loud and also consider either filming yourself or delivering it to a colleague who can offer feedback on style and content. Encourage them to use the Coaching Feedback Form in Appendix 4 in order to help them capture their thoughts and feedback in a structured way.

Organiser / venue checklist:

☐ **Keep in touch with the organiser and the venue.**

☐ **Check out the suitability of the venue and the size of the room** – a room that is too big can be as difficult to deal with as one that is too small. People need some personal space – too little and the audience will be uncomfortable; too much and it will be hard for you to generate a responsive atmosphere.

Be aware, and cater for, delegates with special needs or disabilities.

160

❑ **Confirm your requirements with the venue** – give the hotel a diagram of your room size and layout preferences – ask them to arrange the seating so that the front of the room is the focal point. Ask for as a big a screen as the room will allow and confirm any other technical requirements. Find out:

- when you can have access to the room
- who will be your contact?
- what is their contact number?
- will the room be secure?
- where will breaks be taken?
- will there be water on the tables?

Audience checklist

❑ **Confirm the audience arrangements.**

- Numbers, starting and finishing time.
- Will they need joining instructions or a map?
- Do they have any other special requirements?

Kit checklist

❑ **Carry your own PC, memory stick, data projector and flipchart pens** – with these few essentials, you know that you have everything that you need to run your presentation.

You may also want to carry or organise:

- extension leads and floor tape
- Ipod/MP3 and speakers
- stationery, lapel badges, name cards
- remote control and spare batteries.

The night before the presentation

Prepare yourself physically – have a good night's sleep beforehand and do not be tempted to eat or drink too much.

On the day of the presentation

If you are the only speaker, then you have the opportunity to set the scene for yourself. Consider the room set-up, the ambience and how you will greet each person as they arrive.

❑ **Feel good about yourself.**

❑ **Wear clothes that you feel comfortable in and be an early bird** – arrive well before your audience is due and use this time to set-up the presentation room.

❏ **On arrival, organise the venue** – check the arrangements (signage, room set-up, coffee etc), and the equipment. Confirm where the toilets are, what the fire drill is and what is your responsibility is should there be a fire or other emergency.

- Adjust the air conditioning (open the windows?) to circulate the air.
- Set-up your PC and PowerPoint and put up a welcome slide or prepare a flipchart.
- Set out any handouts.
- Put on some music.

❏ **Organise yourself** – do whatever you have to do to set yourself for success:

- Review your content – glance through your X-ray Sheet once more and write your agenda on to a flipchart.
- Get focused – your positive attitude, energy, preparation and enthusiasm for the subject will be apparent to everyone – stay positive!
- Deal with your nerves – they are caused by adrenalin. Remember, a little is good, too much is not, so burn it off by doing some relaxation, breathing or warm-up exercises (see chapter 4).

❏ **When you begin to present** – use the Ready Position, make eye contact and smile!

Keeping control

It is your responsibility as presenter to set the style, tone and pace of the presentation and to ensure that it runs on track and to time, delivering the content necessary to meet the purpose of the event.

It is much easier and more enjoyable to give a presentation when the audience is comfortable and engaged and all of your pre-work, if carried out effectively, will give you immediate payback. As you present, continue to give your attention to the audience – be aware of their mood and body language and respond as necessary.

Stay positive in your approach and do not be misled by any individual's body language – folded arms may show negativity, or that the person is cold; leaning forward in the chair may show hostility, or deep interest. Look for more general and widespread signals and respond accordingly.

Do not be overly influenced by one or two people's negative body language – you may be such a powerful presenter that you have the ability to make these individuals totally despondent after just three or four minutes, or (more realistically) their attitude may have something to do with what else is going on in their lives, or has happened to them over the previous thirty-five years!

Have confidence and enjoy your presentations!

Appendices

- Appendix 1 – PowerPoint Skills Questionnaire

- Appendix 2 – Adding an Agenda to PowerPoint Slides

- Appendix 3 – Features of PowerPoint 2003

- Appendix 4 – Coaching Feedback Form

- Appendix 5 – Sample of a completed X-ray Sheet

Stand & Deliver

Appendix 1
Powerpoint Skills Questionnaire

Use this Questionnaire to find out about your current technical ability in using Microsoft PowerPoint.

Tick the box that most accurately describes your current level of expertise for each statement on a scale of 1-10, with 10 being the most proficient. You will quickly be able to see areas that you may like to develop.

Microsoft has a comprehensive range of step by step tutorials on each aspect of using PowerPoint.

Refer to **www.office.microsoft.com** and select the Training home page, then scroll down to Browse Training by Product.

Topic	Least Proficient						Most Proficient			
	1	2	3	4	5	6	7	8	9	10
Using the Slide Master										
Working with text boxes										
Creating and modifying bulleted lists										
Inserting Clip Art										
Adapting Clip Art (using Group and Ungroup)										
Inserting Pictures										
Using AutoShapes and other drawing tools										
Inserting and amending Organisation Charts										
Creating and modifying charts in PowerPoint										
Importing charts from Excel										
Importing text from other applications										
Using Microsoft Word Tables within PowerPoint										
Using Slide Sorter View to move, copy and delete slides										
Working in Outline View										
Using *Entrance* custom animation										
Using *Emphasis* custom animation										
Using *Exit* custom animation										
Using *Motion paths* custom animation										
Applying slide transitions to a presentation										
Applying Headers and Footers										
Running and navigating a slide show										
Adding Speaker Notes										
Printing the presentation in different formats										
Looping a presentation										
Applying Design Templates										
Creating your own Design Templates										
Creating and using Custom Shows										
Using Movies in a presentation										
Using Sounds in a presentation										
Creating and using Hyperlinks and Action buttons										
Using Meeting Minder and Action Items										
Setting and rehearsing timings for your slide show										

Appendix 2
Adding an Agenda to Powerpoint Slides

Adding agenda tabs to your PowerPoint slides gives the audience an indication of where you are in your presentation. It serves as a reminder of what has already been covered and what is coming next.

Step 1:

☐ Once you are completely comfortable with the structure of your presentation, write down on a piece of paper the headings that you want to appear on your agenda. These may be the same as the headings on your X-ray sheet.

Use Master View

Step 2:

☐ Open your PowerPoint presentation in Slide Master View.

☐ Add a rectangle to the left hand side or the bottom of the slide. Choose a colour to 'in-fill' the rectangle that complements the background colour of your slides.

☐ Type in your chosen agenda headings that you wrote on the paper in black, white or another strong colour (see Figure 1).

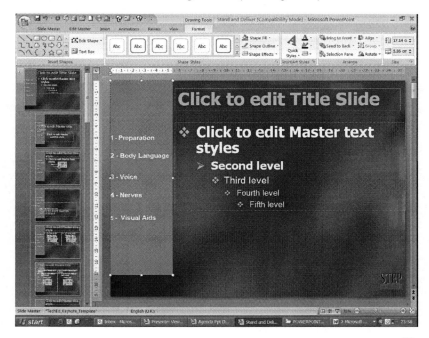

Figure 1

☐ If you now change from Master View to Normal View you will see that all your slides now show your agenda.

Step 3:

This is the tricky part!

☐ Work in Normal View.

☐ Create a text box that will fit over and cover a single agenda heading. Choose a contrasting in-fill colour for the new text box. Copy it onto each slide.

☐ The new text box should be placed over the agenda heading that you wish to highlight. Re-type in the agenda heading that is now covered (see Figure 2).

☐ Repeat for each slide.

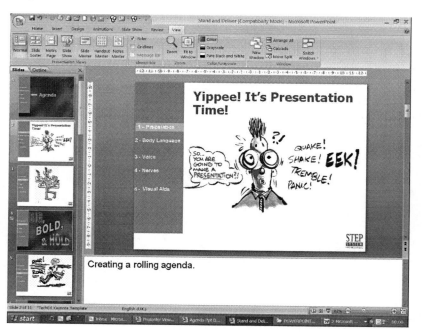

Figure 2

☐ Run your slideshow. The contrasting text boxes will now highlight where you are in your agenda.

Appendix 3
Features of Powerpoint 2003

PowerPoint 2003 has many useful features. Particularly worthy of attention are:

1. Package for CD
2. Speaker Notes
3. Pen Tools
4. Presenter View

1. Package for CD

This feature saves your presentation, along with any linked files and associated objects – for example, video clips or special fonts. It will also include the PowerPoint Viewer, which is a piece of software needed to run your presentation. Using this feature means that nothing has to be installed on a recipient's computer for the presentation to run successfully. Go to: **File**, then select **Package for CD** (see Figure 1).

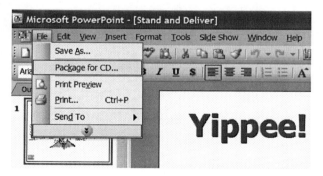

Figure 1

You do not have to save your presentation to a CD, but by clicking the **Copy to Folder** button (see Figure 2), you can save your presentation to any location that you choose and onto a memory stick if you wish.

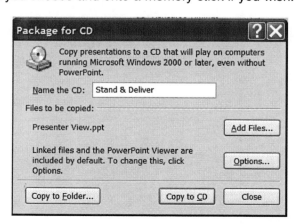

Figure 2

You can also add other presentations to this folder. For example, you may have several versions of the same presentation for different audiences. Simply click the **Add Files** button as you are creating your folder and you can add any other files that you choose.

2. Speaker Notes

It is often necessary to capture live comments, requests, questions or thoughts that arise during a presentation. One way of course, is to use pencil and paper, but an effective alternative is to use Speaker Notes. This is a feature available in PowerPoint that allows you to instantly type in and save any information that you need to record and because it happens live, clearly demonstrates to your audience that you have done it.

To access Speaker Notes, click on the notes icon in the bottom left corner of your screen. This will display a Slides menu (see Figure 3).

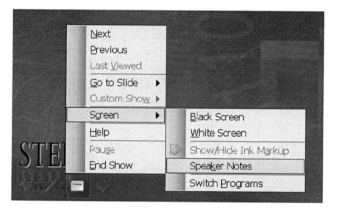

Figure 3

Select **Screen**, click on **Speaker Notes** and a Speaker Notes box will appear (see Figure 4).

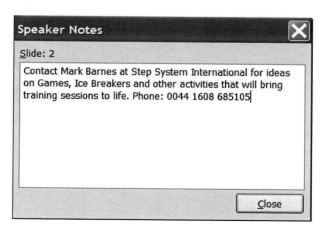

Figure 4

You can now type in any information that you need to remember. When you have finished typing (or writing, if you have a tablet PC), close the window and this information will be saved for your reference after the presentation.

A further advantage of this tool is that the Speaker Notes box will also display any notes that you have written into your slide show before your presentation. To prepare these prompts while working in PowerPoint, select **Normal View**. Underneath each slide, there is an area where you can type your notes.

3. Pen Tools

Consider using a tablet PC with a write-on screen for your presentations, as this will really help to bring your presentation to life. By writing on the screen with the stylus, you can illustrate concepts spontaneously or highlight specific points. (This feature is available on ordinary PC's too, but it takes much more practice to use a mouse to control the writing!)

During your presentation, you can click on the pen icon in the bottom left hand corner of the screen. This will open a pen menu which allows you to select your pen type (Ballpoint, Felt Tip or Highlighter) and the ink colour (see Figure 5).

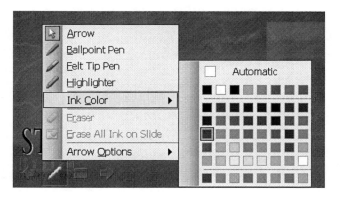

Figure 5

Any annotations that you make will stay with the slide even when you move on to a different one. If these are saved at the end of your presentation, they can form a useful record of the interaction that you have had with your audience, and this is especially useful if you need to draw on that information again, or to circulate it by email.

4. Presenter View

If you have two monitors, for example your PC screen and a data projector, you can display your presentation on one of them and your own notes on the other in **Presenter View** (see Figure 6).

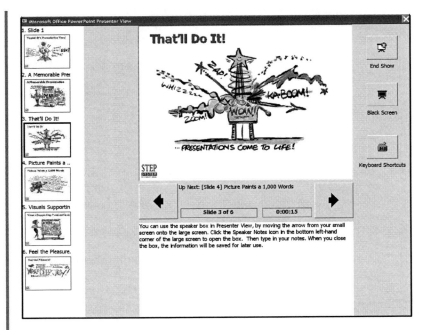

Figure 6

Some advantages of using Presenter View are:

❑ **Presenter View shows thumbnails of your slides** – these are displayed along the left hand edge, so that you can see what is coming next. You can use these to scroll backwards or forwards to select individual slides, allowing you flexibility in the order that you deliver your content should the agenda change, or in response to a question from the audience.

❑ **A clock is displayed to show your elapsed time** – helping you to stay on track and keep control of your time.

❑ **There are controls that will black the screen** – a useful feature that means the audience can focus on what you are saying, rather than on the information displayed on the large screen.

❑ **Your notes are displayed for you** – the font used here is rather small to read during your presentation, so it is better to rely on your X-ray sheet.

Setting up Presenter View:

Step 1. Set up the Monitor:

❑ Right click on your desktop and select **Properties**. A Display Properties box will appear (see Figure 7).

❑ Click the **Settings** tab.

❑ Right click the monitor labelled 2 and select **Attached**.

❑ Select **Extend my Windows desktop onto this monitor**.

❑ Click **OK**.

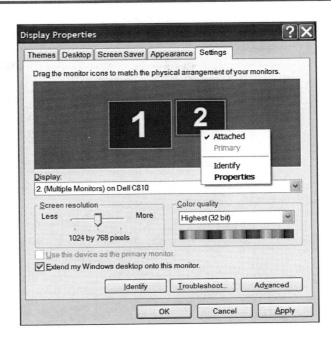

Figure 7

A note of caution: this is not always possible – you will need to experiment with your own equipment.

Step 2. Load the Slideshow:

Open your presentation and select **Slide Show**, then click **Set Up Show** (see Figure 8).

Figure 8

❑   A 'Set Up Show' box will appear (see Figure 9).

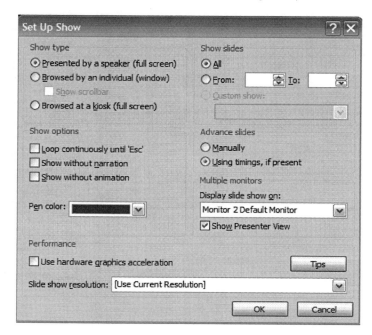

Figure 9

❑   In the multiple monitors section, select **Show Presenter View**.

❑   Click **OK**.

Step 3. Run your Slideshow:

Now when you run your slide show, you will see 2 different views. The audience will see your whole slide as before, whereas you will see 'Presenter View' on your screen (see Figure 6).

Accessing Speaker Notes & Pen Tools in Presenter View

❑   To access the Speaker Notes and Pen Tools features (see earlier in this appendix) during your presentation, you will need to scroll the arrow to the left of your small computer screen until it disappears. The arrow will reappear on the large audience's large screen. You can then use the arrow and your keyboard to access the icons in the bottom left hand corner of the large screen.

It will take practice to feel confident using the 2 screens in this way – experiment to choose which set-up suits you best.

Appendix 4
Coaching Feedback Form

Presentation _____

Body Language	
Eye Contact	
Posture	
Gesture	
Movement	
Facial Expression	
Dress	
Voice	
Volume	
Tone	
Pace	
Pause	
Clarity	
'Non-words'	
Content/Structure	
Introduction	
Clear Map	
Structure	
Flow/Transitions	
Language	
Audience Involvement/Rapport	
Visual Impact	
Question Handling	
Close	
General Comments	

Appendix 5
Example of a completed X-ray sheet

Booklist

Michael Argyle, *'The Psychology of Interpersonal Behaviour'*, Penguin, 1994

Cicely Berry, *'Your Voice and How to Use It'*, Virgin, 2000

Andrew Bradbury, *'Successful Presentation Skills',* Kogan Page, 2006

Bonnie E. Burn, *'Flip Chart Power'*, Pfeiffer & Company

Tony Buzan, *'Use Your Head'* (and others), BBC Books, 1995

Sue Fox, *'Etiquette for Dummies',* Wiley Publishing, 1999

Alastair Grant, *'Presentation Perfect',* The Industrial Society, 1998

Antony Jay & Ros Jay, *'Effective Presentation',* Pitman, 1996

Robert Lowe, *'Improvisation, Inc'*, Jossey-Bass/Pfeiffer, 2000

Albert Mehrabian, *'Silent Messages - Implicit Communication of Emotions and Attitudes'*, Wadsworth, 1981, (Currently distributed by Albert Mehrabian, am@kaaj.com)

Angela Murray, *'Business Presentations',* Teach Yourself Books, Hodder & Stoughton, 1999

Roger von Oech, *'A Whack on the Side of the Head'*, Warner Books, 1998

Jerry Weissman, *'Presenting to Win'*, Pearson Education, 2003

Faithe Wempen, *'PowerPoint, Advanced Presentation Techniques'*, Wiley Publishing, 2004

Index